Envision It! | Visual Skills Handbook

Author's Purpose

Cause and Effect

Classify and Categorize

Compare and Contrast

Details and Facts

Draw Conclusions

Fact and Opinion

Graphic Sources

Main Idea and Details

Sequence

Steps in a Process

Literary Elements

Author's Purpose

Authors write to inform or entertain.

To Inform

To Entertain

Cause and Effect

Cause

Why did it happen?

What happened?

Effect

Classify and Categorize

Which toys belong together?

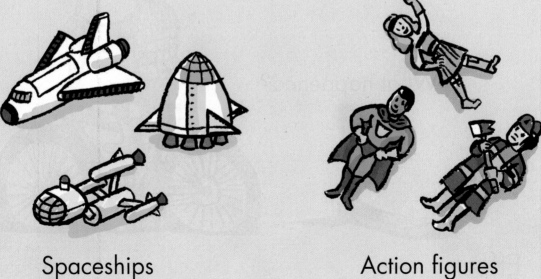

Spaceships   Action figures

Compare and Contrast

How are
we alike?

How are
we different?

Details and Facts

Draw Conclusions

Use what you already know to help you understand what is happening.

Fact and Opinion

A statement of fact can be proven true or false.

A statement of opinion tells someone's ideas or feelings.

Opinion

Graphic Sources

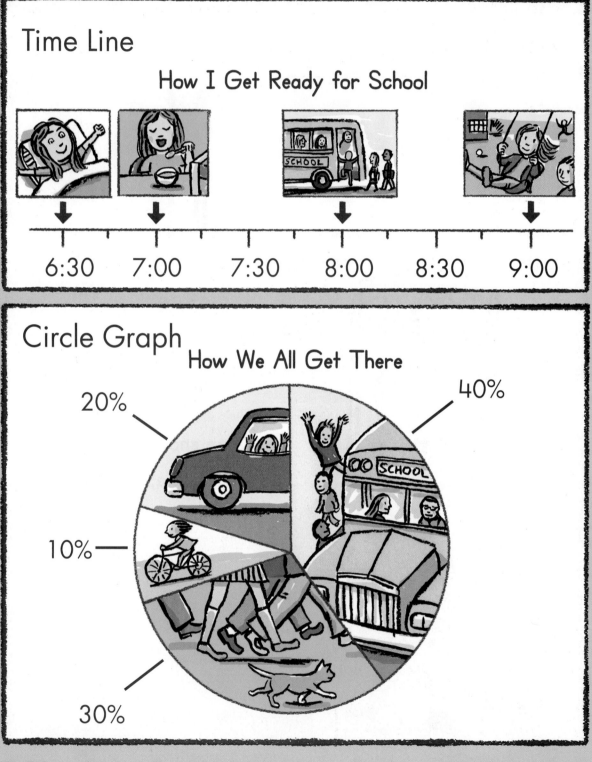

Time Line

How I Get Ready for School

6:30   7:00   7:30   8:00   8:30   9:00

Circle Graph

How We All Get There

20%

40%

10%

30%

Main Idea and Details

Main Idea
What is the selection all about?

Details

Sequence

What happens first, next, and last?

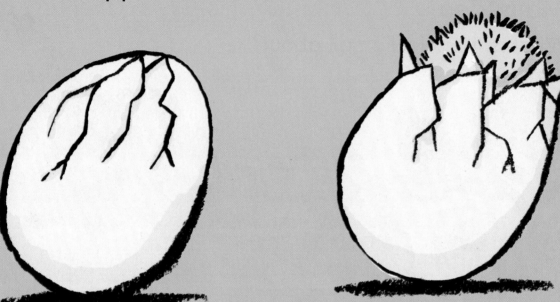

Steps in a Process

1

2

3

4

Literary Elements

Characters

Plot

Beginning   Middle   End

What happens in the beginning, middle, and end of the story?

Problem/Solution

Problem

Solution

Setting

Where and when does the story take place?

Theme

What is the big idea in the story?

Envision It! | Visual Strategies Handbook

Background Knowledge

Important Ideas

Inferring

Monitor and Clarify

Predict and Set Purpose

Questioning

Story Structure

Summarize

Text Structure

Visualize

Background Knowledge

Background knowledge is what you already know about a topic. Use background knowledge before, during, and after reading to monitor your comprehension.

Let's Think About Reading!

When I use background knowledge, I ask myself
- What do I already know?
- What does this remind me of?
- What other stories does this make me think of?

Important Ideas

Important ideas are essential ideas and supporting details in a selection. Important ideas include information and facts that provide clues to the author's purpose.

Let's Think About Reading!

When I identify important ideas, I ask myself
- What are the important facts?
- What do the illustrations and photos show?
- What do diagrams and charts show that might be important?

Inferring

When we **infer** we use background knowledge with clues in the text to come up with our own ideas. We do this to support understanding.

Let's **Think** About **Reading!**

When I infer, I ask myself
- What do I already know?
- How does this help me understand what happened?

Monitor and Clarify

We **monitor** comprehension to make sure our reading makes sense. We **clarify** to find out why we haven't understood. Then we fix up problems.

This is hard to understand. I'll reread to figure it out.

Let's Think About Reading!

When I monitor and clarify, I ask myself
- Do I understand what I'm reading?
- What doesn't make sense?
- How can I fix it?

Predict and Set Purpose

We **predict** to tell what might happen next in a story or article. The prediction is based on what has already happened. We **set a purpose** to guide our reading.

Let's Think About Reading!

When I predict and set a purpose, I ask myself
- What do I already know?
- What do I think will probably happen next?
- What is my purpose for reading?

Questioning

Questioning is asking good questions about important text information. Questioning takes place before, during, and after reading.

How fast *does* it go?

When I question, I ask myself
- What will this be about?
- What does the author mean?
- What questions help me make sense of what I'm reading?

EI•23

Story Structure

Story structure is the arrangement of a story from beginning to end. We use the structure to retell important events in a story.

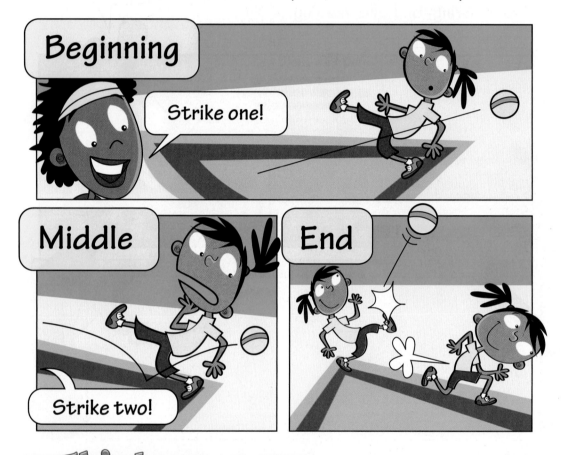

Beginning — Strike one!

Middle — Strike two!

End

Let's Think About Reading!

When I identify story structure, I ask myself
- What happens in the beginning?
- What happens in the middle?
- What happens at the end?
- How can I use this to retell the story?

Summarize

When we **summarize,** we use our own words to retell the most important ideas or events of what we've read. A summary is no more than a few sentences.

Let's Think About Reading!

When I summarize, I ask myself
- What is this mostly about?
- What does the author mean?
- How is the information organized?

Text Structure

We use **text structure** with nonfiction to describe how information is organized, for example, by cause and effect or sequence. Notice text structure before, during, and after reading.

Let's **Think** About **Reading!**

When I identify text structure, I ask myself
- How is the text organized? Cause and effect? Sequence? Others?
- How does structure help me describe the order of the text?

Visualize

When we **visualize**, we form pictures in our minds about what happens in a story or article.

Let's Think About Reading!

When I visualize, I ask myself
- What do I already know?
- Which words and phrases create pictures in my mind?
- How does this help me understand what I'm reading?

SCOTT FORESMAN
READING STREET

GRADE 2

COMMON CORE ©

Program Authors

Peter Afflerbach

Camille Blachowicz

Candy Dawson Boyd

Elena Izquierdo

Connie Juel

Edward Kame'enui

Donald Leu

Jeanne R. Paratore

P. David Pearson

Sam Sebesta

Deborah Simmons

Susan Watts Taffe

Alfred Tatum

Sharon Vaughn

Karen Kring Wixson

Glenview, Illinois

Boston, Massachusetts

Chandler, Arizona

Hoboken, New Jersey

ALWAYS LEARNING

PEARSON

We dedicate Reading Street to
Peter Jovanovich.

His wisdom, courage,
and passion for education
are an inspiration to us all.

Acknowledgments appear on pages 530–531, which constitute an extension of this copyright page.

ISBN-13: 978-0-328-72449-9
ISBN-10:   0-328-72449-1
10 11 12 13 14 15 16 17 18 V057 18 17 16 15

Dear Reader,

A new school year is beginning. Are you ready? You are about to take a trip along a famous street—*Scott Foresman Reading Street*. During this trip you will travel in space with some astronauts. You will explore the desert. You will go camping with Henry and his big dog Mudge. You will even build a robot with good friends Pearl and Wagner.

As you read these stories and articles, you will learn new things that will help you in science and social studies.

While you are enjoying these exciting pieces of literature, you will find that something else is going on— you are becoming a better reader.

Have a great trip, and don't forget to write!

Sincerely,
The Authors

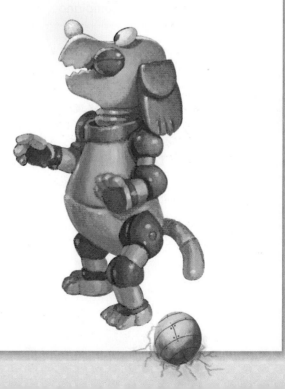

Unit 1 Contents

Exploration

What can we learn from exploring new places and things?

Unit 1 Contents

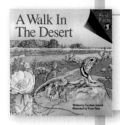

Week 6

Envision It! A Comprehension Handbook

Unit 2 Contents

How can we work together?

WORKING Together

Week 1

Week 2

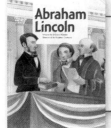
Week 3

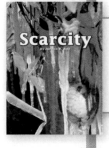

Unit 2 Contents

Week 6

Interactive Review

Envision It! A Comprehension Handbook

Envision It! Visual Skills Handbook EI•1– EI•15

Envision It! Visual Strategies Handbook EI•17– EI•27

Unit 3 Contents

What does it mean to be creative?

Creative Ideas

Week 2

Week 3

Unit 3 Contents

Week 4

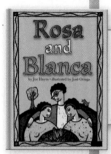
Week 5

Week 6

Interactive Review
Reader's and Writer's Notebook 253–284

Envision It! A Comprehension Handbook

Envision It! Visual Skills
Handbook EI•1–EI•15

Envision It! Visual Strategies
Handbook EI•17–EI•27

Don Leu
The Internet Guy

Right before our eyes, the nature of reading and learning is changing. The Internet and other technologies create new opportunities, new solutions, and new literacies. New reading comprehension skills are required online. They are increasingly important to our students and our society.

Those of us on the Reading Street team are here to help you on this new, and very exciting, journey.

See It!

- **Big Question Video**

- **Concept Talk Video**

- **Envision It! Animations**

- **eReaders**

- **Interactive Sound-Spelling Cards**

butterfly

b

Hear It!

- *Sing with Me* Animations

- eSelections

- **Grammar Jammer**

- **Vocabulary Activities**

The dogs run and bark.
The duck flew.
The dog is running.
The dog is tired.

www.ReadingStreet.com

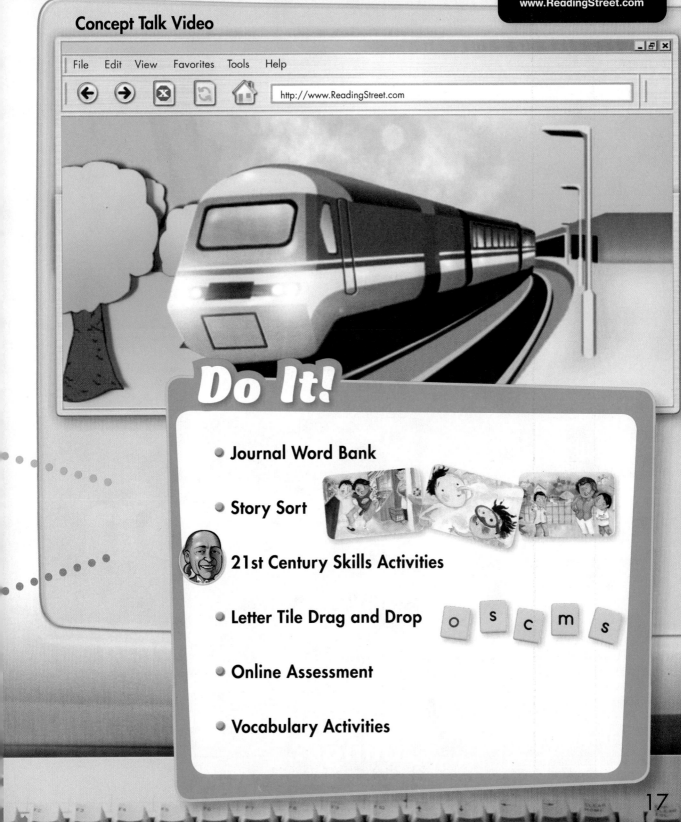

File   Edit   View   Favorites   Tools   Help

http://www.ReadingStreet.com

Do It!

- **Journal Word Bank**

- **Story Sort**

- **21st Century Skills Activities**

- **Letter Tile Drag and Drop**

- **Online Assessment**

- **Vocabulary Activities**

Exploration

What can we learn from exploring new places and things?

THE BIG
?

Let's Talk About

Different Communities

- Share information about different communities.

- Share ideas about how different communities are alike.

READING STREET ONLINE
CONCEPT TALK VIDEO
www.ReadingStreet.com

You will learn
2 4 1
Amazing Words ⭐
this year!

21

Common Core State Standards
Spiral Review Foundational Skills 2.
Demonstrate understanding of spoken
words, syllables, and sounds (phonemes).

Let's Listen for

Sounds

- Find three things that contain the short *o* sound.

- Find something that rhymes with *wag*. Say the sound in the middle of the word.

- Now change that middle sound to short *u*. Say the new word.

**READING STREET ONLINE
SOUND-SPELLING CARDS**
www.ReadingStreet.com

Grocery

$

Fine Jewelry

SALE

Newspaper

23

Common Core State Standards
Foundational Skills 3. Know and apply grade-level phonics and word analysis skills in decoding words.
Also Foundational Skills 3.a., 3.f.

astronaut

a

butterfly

b

elephant

e

tomato

t

octopus

o

READING STREET ONLINE
SOUND-SPELLING CARDS
www.ReadingStreet.com

Phonics

Short Vowels and Consonants

Words I Can Blend

t e l l

g r a b

b a s k e t

g e t

t o p

Sentences I Can Read

1. Tell Matt he must grab it.

2. Drop it in his basket.

3. Tess will get the doll on top.

I Can Read!

Tim and Mom live somewhere in the country. Tim must get his bus in front of the house of a friend. Today, Tim must run to get his bus. Will he miss it? Yes, Tim will miss his bus. Mom said, "It will not do. Tim must have a plan." Mom is someone who can drop a hint. Mom will tell Tim before bed, "Get your backpack and fill it, Tim. Get everything set. I will help you get up early." Mom does get Tim up early. Tim is set. It is beautiful. Tim will not miss his bus.

You've learned

👁 Short Vowels and Consonants

High-Frequency Words
beautiful   country   friend
front   someone   somewhere

The Twin Club

written by Ina Cumpiano
illustrated by Jana Christy

Realistic fiction tells about made-up events that could happen in real life. Now read about two cousins from different communities who enjoy their summers together.

Question of the Week

What can we learn by exploring different communities?

One day last summer, a lady said to us,
"Twins! How cute!"

Jorge put a silly look on his face and I tried
very hard not to roll my eyes.

28

Jorge and I are not twins. We are not even brothers. We're cousins. We are best friends.
But the lady called us twins. We could start a club. It would be the Twin Club!

Even before we were the Twin Club, we
stayed all summer with Grandma Inés. We
did everything together.

Now we were the Twin Club. We had a secret handshake. We built a clubhouse. It was big. But it was hard for both of us to fit.

And, as Twins, we made a promise. "We'll always, always be friends," we told each other.

Together, we walked around Grandma's beautiful small town. We did tricks in front of stores.

Someone, somewhere might have a better club than ours. But I don't think so!

Then one day, Grandma said, "I have news.
The summer is almost over, *chicos*," she said.
"It's time for you to go home to your parents."

It was too soon for the summer to end!
"Jorge and I won't live here again until next
summer, Grandma. We won't be the Twin Club
anymore. Will we?"

"Juan Ramón, your parents miss you very much. They are looking forward to having you back on the farm. And soon you will start second grade. School will be fun!" Grandma Inés said.

Oh, no, it won't, I thought.

We knew it really was both good news and bad news. We would be with our families and friends again, which was good. But Jorge and I would not be together, which was bad. Very, very bad.

Grandma was right. Being back home on our farm was great. The first day back, I went for a walk to our neighbor's barn.

I climbed a ladder in the barn and jumped into the soft hay. I said hello to the goat. The old goose chased me!

That night, I watched fireflies in the meadow.

I thought about the Twin Club when Papi drove me to the bus stop in the morning. I thought about the Twin Club during the bus ride to school. It was a really long ride.

I thought about the Twin Club when I picked
fruit off our trees and when I watched fireflies.
I thought about the Twin Club all the time.

Then, one day, I got an e-mail message.
It was from Jorge.

To: JuanRamon@farmz.com
From: Jorge@ramirez.com
Subject: Hello, Twin Club

Hi Twin,

How are you?
Today, I walked around my neighborhood.
I love to walk around my neighborhood.
I see lots of people, lots of cars, lots of stores.
Everything goes so fast!
I walk to school by myself. My school is two
blocks away.
My friend, Jamilla, and I play basketball in the
park. Sometimes we go to the supermarket
to buy fruit from around the world. AMAZING!
I am glad to be back home, but I miss our
Twin Club!

Your twin cousin,
Jorge

Jorge

I still missed Jorge. But I remembered
what I liked about my home in the country.
Jorge remembered he liked walking in his
neighborhood.

And do you know what was even more fun?
Changing our club name to "The AMAZING
E-mail Twins"!

Now we write to each other about everything.
And we are making plans for next summer at
Grandma's!

Common Core State Standards
Literature 1. Ask and answer such questions as *who, what, where, when, why,* and *how* to demonstrate understanding of key details in a text. **Also Literature 2.**

Think Critically

1. Do you know someone who lives far away? How can you communicate with that person? **Text to Self**

2. What lesson is the author trying to teach with this story?

Author's Purpose

3. Who are the characters in the story? How are they alike and different? Where does the story take place? **Character and Setting**

4. Did anything about this story confuse you? What did you do about it? **Monitor and Clarify**

5. Look Back and Write
Look back at page 33. What is the news the "twins" receive? How do they feel about it? Provide evidence to support your answer.

Key Ideas and Details • Text Evidence

Ina Cumpiano

Ina Cumpiano is a Puerto Rican poet and translator. She lives in a busy San Francisco neighborhood and has written nearly twenty books for children.

Ms. Cumpiano has had many different jobs, but so far her favorite has been being a grandmother for her ten grandchildren.

Jana Christy

Jana Christy once wrote a comic book, but her usual work is illustrating books for children. Ms. Christy lives in Massachusetts with her husband and two sons.

Here are other books written by Ina Cumpiano or illustrated by Jana Christy.

Use the Reading Log in the *Reader's and Writer's Notebook* to record your independent reading.

45

Common Core State Standards
Writing 3. Write narratives in which they recount a well-elaborated event or short sequence of events, include details to describe actions, thoughts, and feelings, use temporal words to signal event order, and provide a sense of closure.
Also Language 1., 2.

Let's Write It!

Key Features of a Personal Narrative

- is about a real experience in the writer's life

- tells a story using the words *I* and *me*

- provides details to make the event vivid

READING STREET ONLINE
GRAMMER JAMMER
www.ReadingStreet.com

Personal Narrative

A **personal narrative** is a story about something that happened to the writer. The student model on the next page is an example of a personal narrative.

Writing Prompt Think about what people learn by exploring a new place. Now write a personal narrative about a new place that you have visited.

Writer's Checklist

Remember, you should . . .

☑ tell about an interesting experience in your life.

☑ use the words *I* and *me*.

☑ use complete sentences.

☑ end sentences with correct punctuation.

Trip to Florida

Last summer my family went to Florida. I got to go to the beach for the first time.

The ocean was beautiful. It was dark blue and clear. My sister and I went swimming. The waves made standing up hard. It was so fun.

After that, we built a sandcastle. It was almost as tall as me! Little by little, the ocean came in and knocked our castle down.

Writing Trait Conventions
Sentences are punctuated correctly with periods.

Genre
A **personal narrative** uses the words *I* and *me*.

Each **sentence** tells a complete idea.

Conventions

Sentences

Remember A **sentence** is a group of words that tells a complete idea. A sentence begins with a capital letter. Many sentences end with a **period**.

47

Social Studies in Reading

Genre
Poetry

- Poetry shows lines of words that have rhythm.

- Poetry often rhymes and often uses repetition to create images.

- Poetry helps you think about what you sense and feel.

- Humorous poems can make you laugh or just smile a little.

- Read "The 1st Day of School" and "The 179th Day of School." Listen for what makes them poetry. Be ready to talk about the rhyme, rhythm, and repetition.

The 1st Day of School

By Jenny Whitehead

Brand-new crayons and
   unchipped chalk.
Brand-new haircut,
   spotless smock.
Brand-new rules—
   "No running, please."
Brand-new pair of
   nervous knees.
Brand-new faces,
   unclogged glue.
Brand-new hamster,
   shiny shoes.
Brand-new teacher,
   classroom fun.
Brand-new school year's
   just begun.

The 179th Day of School

By Jenny Whitehead

Broken crayons and
    mop-head hair.
Scuffed-up shoes and
    squeaky chair.
Dried-up paste,
    chewed, leaky pens.
Dusty chalkboard,
    lifelong friends.
One inch taller,
    bigger brain.
Well-worn books,
    old grape-juice stain.
Paper airplanes,
    classroom cheer.
School is done and
    summer's here!

Let's Think About...

What words **repeat** in "The 1st Day of School"? What do you see when you hear them?

Let's Think About...

How are the settings of the two poems alike and different?

Let's Think About...

Reading Across Texts How are Juan and Jorge from *The Twin Club* like the children in the poems?

Writing Across Texts What would Jorge tell Juan about his first day of school? Use the ideas in the poems. Write an e-mail to Juan about the first day of school.

Common Core State Standards
Foundational Skills 4.b. Read on-level text orally with accuracy, appropriate rate, and expression on successive readings. **Also Foundational Skills 4., Speaking/Listening 1., 6.**

Let's **Learn** It!

Vocabulary

To **alphabetize** words means to put them in order of the letters of the alphabet.

Practice It! Read these words. Write them in alphabetical order.

sun wet home
bus morning ride

Fluency

Read with Appropriate Rate

Read as if you are speaking. Slow down if you do not understand what you read.

Practice It! Read the sentences below with a partner.

1. Jan and Erin are friends.

2. See the house on the hill.

3. At night, the beautiful stars shine.

50

Listening and Speaking

Speak to share ideas and information, and listen to hear questions.

Why We Speak and Why We Listen

We speak to share ideas and information. We also speak to ask and answer questions. Listen carefully to others when they speak. We listen to hear questions. We also listen to hear ideas and information.

Practice It! Think of what you like about a family member. Tell other students about it. Be sure to speak clearly and slowly. Speak in complete sentences.

Tips

Listening ...

• Be ready to ask relevant questions.

Speaking ...

• Speak clearly at an appropriate pace.

Common Core State Standards

Language 6. Use words and phrases acquired through conversations, reading and being read to, and responding to texts, including using adjectives and adverbs to describe (e.g., *When other kids are happy that makes me happy*).
Also Speaking/Listening 1.

Let's Talk About

Space Exploration

- Share information about how astronauts explore space.

- Share ideas about what equipment is required.

READING STREET ONLINE
CONCEPT TALK VIDEO
www.ReadingStreet.com

52

Common Core State Standards
Spiral Review Foundational Skills 2.
Demonstrate understanding of spoken
words, syllables, and sounds (phonemes).

Phonemic Awareness

Let's Listen for

Sounds

● Find five things that contain a long vowel sound.

● Find the plane. Change the long *a* sound in plane to a short *a* sound. Say the new word.

● Find something that rhymes with *like*. Say the sound in the middle of that word.

● Find the rose. Say the sound in the middle of *rose*.

READING STREET ONLINE
SOUND-SPELLING CARDS
www.ReadingStreet.com

54

55

Common Core State Standards
Foundational Skills 3.c. Decode regularly spelled two-syllable words with long vowels. **Also Foundational Skills 3., 3.f.**

Envision It! | **Sounds to Know**

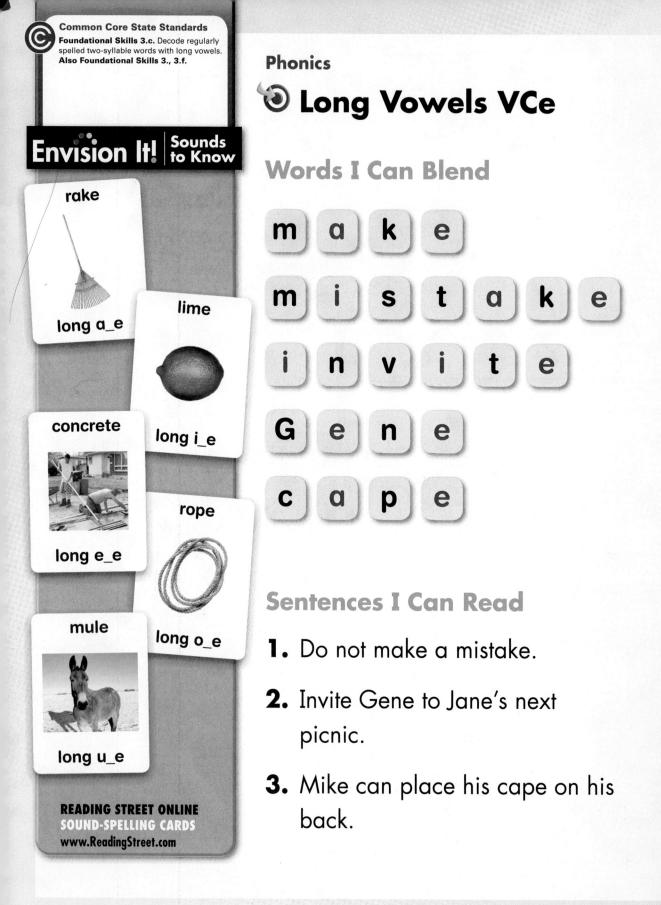

rake
long a_e

lime
long i_e

concrete
long e_e

rope
long o_e

mule
long u_e

READING STREET ONLINE
SOUND-SPELLING CARDS
www.ReadingStreet.com

Phonics

🔊 Long Vowels VCe

Words I Can Blend

m a k e

m i s t a k e

i n v i t e

G e n e

c a p e

Sentences I Can Read

1. Do not make a mistake.

2. Invite Gene to Jane's next picnic.

3. Mike can place his cape on his back.

I Can Read!

Dave and Grace live close together. They like the game Space Home. It is a fun game for Dave and Grace. Space Home can work like this. It must take place in another time. Machines move people from everywhere in the world into space. A man or a woman in the game will race to make new friends. It is a nice game. Dave and Grace invite a classmate to use this game with them.

You've learned

👁 Long Vowels VCe

High-Frequency Words

everywhere   live   machines
move   woman   work   world

Exploring Space

with an Astronaut

by Patricia J. Murphy

Genre

Expository text tells facts about a topic. Next you will read facts about the crew of a real space shuttle.

What can we learn by exploring space?

Lift-off!

3 . . . 2 . . . 1 . . . Lift-off!
A space shuttle climbs high into the sky. Inside the shuttle, astronauts are on their way to learn more about space.

What is an astronaut?

An astronaut is a person who goes into space. Astronauts fly on a space shuttle.

The space shuttle takes off like a rocket. It lands like an airplane.

United States

Meet Eileen Collins.

Eileen Collins is an astronaut. She was the first woman to be a space shuttle pilot. She was also the first woman to be the leader of a space shuttle trip.

She and four other astronauts worked as a team. Some astronauts flew the space shuttle. Others did experiments.

How do astronauts live in space?

In the space shuttle, astronauts float everywhere. Sleeping bags are tied to walls. Toilets have a type of seat belt.

Astronauts exercise to stay strong. They take sponge baths to keep clean.

Why do astronauts go into space?

Astronauts test ways to live and work in a world that is very different from Earth. In space, there is no up and down, no air, and the sun always shines.

Astronauts do experiments. They look for problems and fix them. This will make space travel safer.

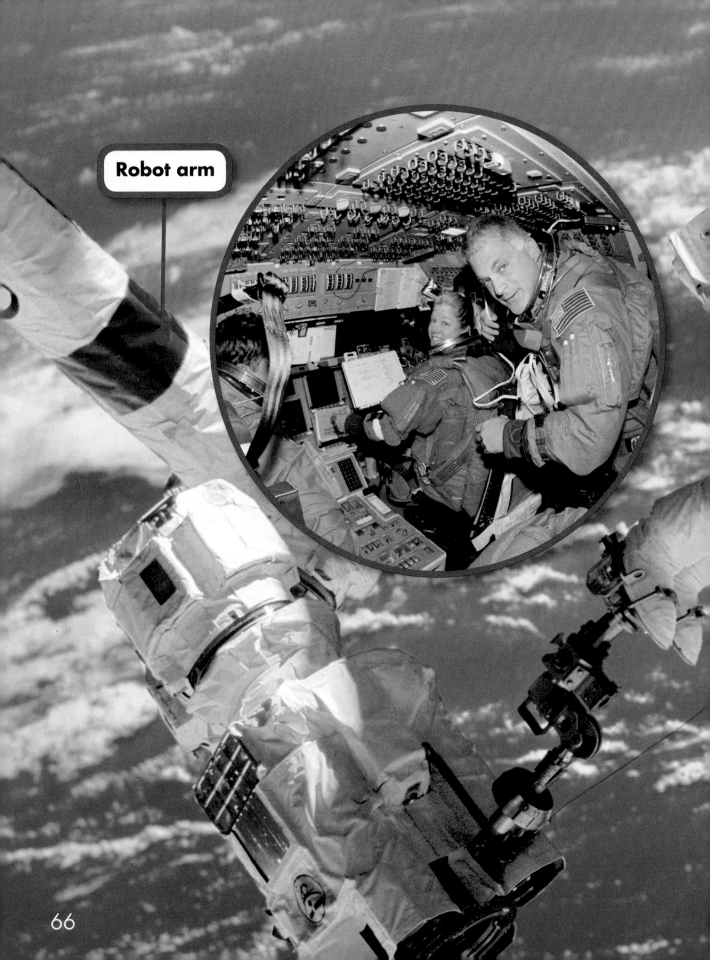

Robot arm

Space suit

What tools do astronauts use?

A space shuttle is a giant toolbox!
It holds tools, such as computers, that
help fly the space shuttle.

Astronauts use robot arms to move
things and people outside the shuttle.
On space walks, space suits keep
astronauts safe.

67

X-ray telescope named *Chandra*

X-ray telescope

Space shuttle

The crew's special job

Eileen Collins and her crew had a special job to do. They took an X-ray telescope into space with them.

First, they tested the telescope. Next, they flipped some switches and let the telescope go into space. Then, the telescope used its rockets to fly higher into space.

Did the astronauts do other jobs too?

Yes. They did experiments with plants and exercise machines. They were studying life without gravity.

When there was some time to rest, the astronauts could look out their window. They saw Earth from many, many miles away!

Rocky Mountains in Colorado

Plant experiment

69

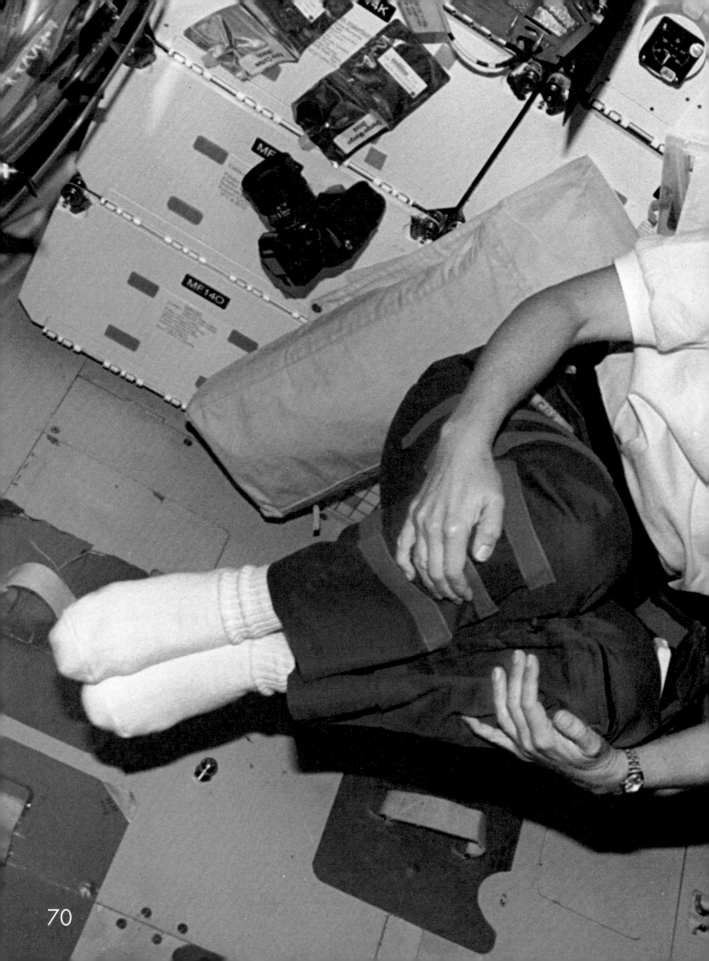

Would you like to fly into space?

Do you like math and science? Do you like to visit new places? Do you like fast roller coasters? Astronauts do too! Maybe someday you will become an astronaut, just like Eileen Collins.

Common Core State Standards

Informational Text 1. Ask and answer such questions as *who, what, where, when, why,* and *how* to demonstrate understanding of key details in a text. **Also Informational Text 5., 6.**

Envision It! Retell

Think Critically

1. How is being an astronaut different from other kinds of jobs? How is it the same?

Text to World

2. Why do you think the author asks whether you would like to fly in space? *Author's Purpose*

3. What is the most important thing the author wanted you to know? How can you tell it apart from the topic?

Main Idea and Details

4. Find a heading on one of the pages. What does the heading say? How do headings help you as you read? *Text Structure*

5. Look Back and Write
Look back at pages 68–69. Do all astronauts do the same jobs? Provide evidence to support your answer.

Key Ideas and Details • Text Evidence

Patricia J. Murphy

Patricia Murphy likes everything about writing a book. When she starts a new book, she says, it's "fun and scary." When she's in the middle, her days are filled with "unexpected adventure and surprises—and a lot of mess and hard work." In the end, when a book is written, she feels excited and a little sad that it's all over. Then it's on to the next book!

Ms. Murphy is a writer and a photographer. She lives in Illinois.

Here are other books by Patricia J. Murphy.

A TRUE BOOK
TASTE
Patricia J. Murphy

A TRUE BOOK
TOUCH
Patricia J. Murphy

Use the Reading Log in the *Reader's and Writer's Notebook* to record your independent reading.

73

Common Core State Standards
Writing 2. Write informative/explanatory texts in which they introduce a topic, use facts and definitions to develop points, and provide a concluding statement or section. **Also Writing 8., Language 1.**

Expository

Let's Write It!

Key Features of Expository Nonfiction

- gives information about a topic
- tells about real people, places, and events
- uses facts and details

READING STREET ONLINE
GRAMMAR JAMMER
www.ReadingStreet.com

Expository Nonfiction
Expository nonfiction tells facts about a topic. The student model on the next page is an example of expository nonfiction.

Writing Prompt Think about what scientists have learned from exploring space. Now write a paragraph telling something you have learned about space.

Writer's Checklist

Remember, you should ...

☑ tell about real people, places, or events.

☑ use different kinds of sentences.

☑ make sure every sentence has a subject.

74

Astronauts in Space

The astronauts who travel in space have different jobs. Some fly the space craft, and others do experiments.

They have to fix problems. They study life without gravity. Being an astronaut is hard work! Would you like to be an astronaut?

Genre
Expository nonfiction
tells about real people, places, or events.

Each sentence has a **subject.**

Writing Trait Sentences
The writer uses different kinds of sentences.

Conventions

Subjects

Remember A sentence's **subject** tells who or what does something.

An astronaut goes into space.

75

Common Core State Standards
Informational Text 2. Identify the main topic of a multiparagraph text as well as the focus of specific paragraphs within the text. **Also Informational Text 5., 9.**

Genre
Expository Text

- Expository text explains an object or idea.

- Expository text gives facts and details.

- An article with graphic features may be expository text.

- Read "A Trip to Space Camp." Look for elements that make this article expository text.

A Trip to Space Camp

by Ann Weil

What does it feel like to go into space? Would you like to find out? Then maybe space camp is for you!

There are all sorts of space camps that you could try. Some are for adults. Some are for teens. There is even a space camp for children as young as seven years old. It is called Parent-Child Space Camp. Parent-Child Space Camp takes place over a long weekend. Families can go to Space Camp together.

Let's Think About...

How old do you have to be to go to Parent-Child Space Camp?
Expository Text

MISSION SCIENTIST   ORBITER SYSTEMS OFFICER   FLIGHT

Let's **Think** About...

This page tells about machines used in Space Camp. Name one of the machines and tell what it does.
Expository Text

Space Camp uses some of the same machines used to train real astronauts. There's a special chair that makes you feel like you are walking on the moon. Another chair is like the kind that astronauts use when they go outside their rocket ship to fix something. A third kind of chair makes you feel like you're floating in space. Still another machine spins you in circles and flips you head over heels. Then there's the Space Shot. The Space Shot shoots you straight into the air at about forty-five to fifty miles per hour. You fall back down just as fast. Then you bump up and down a few times before it's over.

Y6 gravity chair

Working in space

78

A multi-axis giro

Everyone at Space Camp works together on special missions. On these missions you'll do work like real astronauts do in space. You might get to fly a rocket ship. It's only pretend, of course. You won't really fly into space. But it looks and feels like the real thing. And that's really fun!

Moon gravity chair

Let's Think About...

Reading Across Texts Both selections talk about astronauts. What do you learn about astronauts in the selections?

Writing Across Texts How is going to Space Camp like being an astronaut? How is it different? Write a sentence telling about one similarity. Write a sentence telling about one difference.

Common Core State Standards
Foundational Skills 4.b. Read on-level text orally with accuracy, appropriate rate, and expression on successive readings.
Also Speaking/Listening 1.a.

Let's Learn It!

Vocabulary

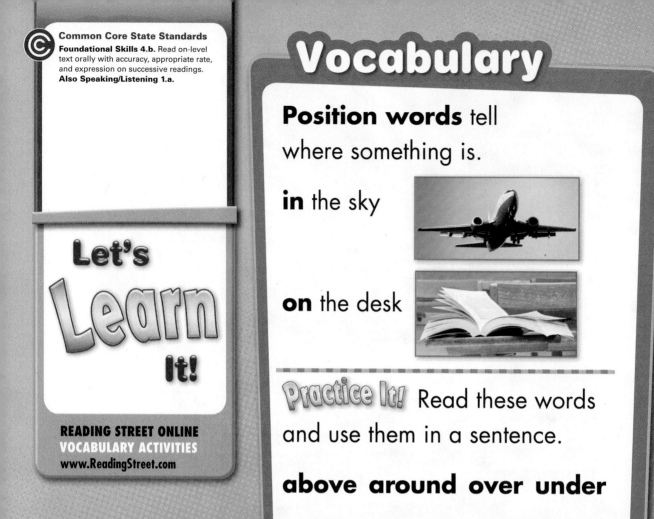

Position words tell where something is.

in the sky

on the desk

Practice It! Read these words and use them in a sentence.

above   around   over   under

Fluency

Read with Accuracy

When you read, blend each word you see. Check new words in the sentence to make sure they make sense. Look for word parts to help you understand new words.

Practice It!

1. The sun is a big star.

2. Astronauts work in space.

3. Sometimes the moon looks like a big ball.

Listening and Speaking

Speak clearly. Be sure others can hear you.

Be a Good Speaker

When speaking to others, speak slowly and carefully. Stand or sit up straight. Speak loudly enough so others can hear. Be sure to listen carefully when others speak.

Practice It! Tell the class which picture you like the most from *Exploring Space with an Astronaut*. Explain why you like that picture. Take turns and speak clearly. Listen carefully when others speak.

Tips

Listening ...

• Listen to each speaker.

Speaking ...

• Share information and your ideas about the topic.

Teamwork ...

• Take turns speaking.

81

Common Core State Standards

Language 6. Use words and phrases acquired through conversations, reading and being read to, and responding to texts, including using adjectives and adverbs to describe (e.g., *When other kids are happy that makes me happy*).
Also Speaking/Listening 1.

Let's Talk About

Exploring Nature

- Share information about exploring nature.

- Share ideas about what is explored in nature.

READING STREET ONLINE
CONCEPT TALK VIDEO
www.ReadingStreet.com

82

Common Core State Standards
Spiral Review Foundational Skills 2.
Demonstrate understanding of spoken
words, syllables, and sounds (phonemes).

Phonemic Awareness

Let's Listen for

Sounds

- Find two words that rhyme with *pant.*

- Find two things that begin with the /th/ /r/ blend. Say each word.

- A skunk has a white stripe. Say each sound in the word *stripe.*

READING STREET ONLINE
SOUND-SPELLING CARDS
www.ReadingStreet.com

Common Core State Standards

Foundational Skills 3. Know and apply grade-level phonics and word analysis skills in decoding words. **Also Foundational Skills 3.f.**

Envision It! | Sounds to Know

splash

spl

strawberry

str

Phonics

Consonant Blends

Words I Can Blend

p l a n t

s t r i p e

s p r a n g

s t r u c k

s p l e n d i d

Sentences I Can Read

1. His plant has a wide stripe.

2. Nick sprang up when Lin struck the bell.

3. Our class has a splendid rule.

I Can Read!

Ann and Dan got a pup. Bear is the pup. Ann and Dan love that pup. Bear is tan and has a black stripe on his back. That pup can build a big mess. Mother and Father had a splendid plant. Once an ant from that plant went straight on that pup's nose. Bear struck at that ant, but he couldn't get it. He struck his nose instead. Bear fell on the plant and that plant went everywhere. What a mess!

You've learned

◎ Consonant Blends

High-Frequency Words
bear   build   couldn't   father
love   mother   straight

87

Henry and Mudge

and the Starry Night

by Cynthia Rylant
illustrated by Suçie Stevenson

Genre

Realistic fiction tells about made-up events that could happen in real life. Next, read about Henry and his dog, Mudge, and their camping trip.

Question of the Week

What can we discover by exploring nature?

Contents

Big Bear Lake

In August Henry and Henry's big dog Mudge always went camping. They went with Henry's parents.

Henry's mother had been a Camp Fire Girl, so she knew all about camping.

She knew how to set up a tent.

She knew how to build a campfire. She knew how to cook camp food.

Henry's dad didn't know anything about camping. He just came with a guitar and a smile.

Henry and Mudge loved camping. This year they were going to Big Bear Lake, and Henry couldn't wait.

"We'll see deer, Mudge," Henry said.
Mudge wagged.

"We'll see raccoons," said Henry.
Mudge shook Henry's hand.

"We might even see a *bear*," Henry said. Henry was not so sure he wanted to see a bear. He shivered and put an arm around Mudge.

Mudge gave a big, slow, *loud* yawn. He drooled on Henry's foot.

Henry giggled. "No bear will get *us*, Mudge," Henry said. "We're too *slippery!*"

A Good Smelly Hike

Henry and Mudge and Henry's parents drove to Big Bear Lake. They parked the car and got ready to hike.

Everyone had a backpack, even Mudge. (His had lots of crackers.) Henry's mother said, "Let's go!" And off they went.

They walked and walked and climbed and
climbed. It was beautiful.

Henry saw a fish jump straight out of a stream.
He saw a doe and her fawn. He saw waterfalls
and a rainbow.

Mudge didn't see much of anything. He was smelling. Mudge loved to hike and smell. He smelled a raccoon from yesterday. He smelled a deer from last night.

He smelled an oatmeal cookie from Henry's back pocket. "Mudge!" Henry laughed, giving Mudge the cookie.

Finally Henry's mother picked a good place to camp.

Henry's parents set up the tent. Henry
unpacked the food and pans and lanterns. Mudge
unpacked a ham sandwich. Finally, the camp was
almost ready. It needed just one more thing:
"Who knows the words to 'Love Me Tender'?"
said Henry's father with a smile, pulling out his
guitar. Henry looked at Mudge and groaned.

Green Dreams

It was a beautiful night.

Henry and Henry's parents lay on their backs by the fire and looked at the sky. Henry didn't know there were so many stars in the sky.

"There's the Big Dipper," said Henry's mother.

"There's the Little Dipper," said Henry.

"There's E. T.," said Henry's dad.

Mudge wasn't looking at stars. He was chewing on a log. He couldn't get logs this good at home. Mudge loved camping.

Henry's father sang one more sappy love song, then everyone went inside the tent to sleep. Henry's father and mother snuggled. Henry and Mudge snuggled.

It was as quiet as quiet could be. Everyone slept safe and sound, and there were no bears, no scares. Just the clean smell of trees . . . and wonderful green dreams.

Common Core State Standards
Literature 1. Ask and answer such questions as *who, what, where, when, why,* and *how* to demonstrate understanding of key details in a text. **Also Literature 7.**

Think Critically

1. Would you rather go camping with Henry's mother or Henry's father? Explain your answer. **Text to Self**

2. What does the author think of camping? How do you know? **Author's Purpose**

3. What is the setting for this story? What are some things the characters see and smell in this setting? **Character and Setting**

4. Use the pictures on this page to retell the story. **Story Structure**

5. Look Back and Write
Look back at page 101. What are the Big Dipper and the Little Dipper? Provide evidence to support your answer.

Key Ideas and Details • Text Evidence

Meet the Author and the Illustrator

Cynthia Rylant

Cynthia Rylant never read books when she was young. There was no library in her town. After college, Ms. Rylant worked in a library. "Within a few weeks, I fell in love with children's books," she says. She has written more than 60 books!

Suçie Stevenson

Suçie Stevenson has drawn pictures for most of the Henry and Mudge books. Her brother's Great Dane, Jake, was her inspiration for Mudge.

Read these other books by Cynthia Rylant.

Poppleton Forever

Mr. Putter and Tabby Stir the Soup

Reading Log

Describe what is alike and different about the settings and characters in the books you read by Cynthia Rylant.

105

Common Core State Standards
Writing 3. Write narratives in which they recount a well-elaborated event or short sequence of events, include details to describe actions, thoughts, and feelings, use temporal words to signal event order, and provide a sense of closure. **Also Language 1.**

Let's **Write** It!

Key Features of Realistic Fiction

- tells about made-up people and events

- story events could really happen

- story has a beginning, middle, and end

READING STREET ONLINE
GRAMMAR JAMMER
www.ReadingStreet.com

Realistic Fiction

Realistic fiction tells about made-up events that could really happen. The student model on the next page is an example of realistic fiction.

Writing Prompt Think about things that can be discovered in nature. Now write a realistic story about a child who discovers something outdoors.

Writer's Checklist

Remember, you should . . .

☑ tell about events that could happen in real life.

☑ write the beginning, middle, and end.

☑ make sentences complete by including predicates.

A Day at the Beach

Luke went to the beach on a hot summer day. He splashed in the cool water. He dug in the warm sand.

Luke discovered a small pool full of starfish. He left them alone.

He found a smooth rock. He took his rock home to remind him of the day.

Genre Realistic fiction happens in a setting that seems real.

Each sentence has a **predicate**.

Writing Trait Organization The story has a beginning, a middle, and an **end.**

Conventions

Predicates

Remember The **predicate** tells what the subject of the sentence does or is.

Henry **walked home.**

107

Science in Reading

Genre
Procedural Text

- Procedural text gives directions on how to do something one step at a time.

- Procedural text usually has graphic features that help tell how to do something.

- Read "How to Make a S'more." Look for elements of procedural text.

How to Make a S'more

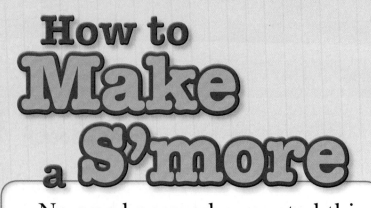

No one knows who created this treat first, but the earliest s'more recipe can be found in the Girl Scouts handbook of 1927. S'more stands for "some more," as in "give me some more." The traditional s'more is made with marshmallows, graham crackers, and a few pieces of chocolate.

Please have an adult assist you when you make this tasty outdoor treat inside.

What You Need:

microwave

1 whole graham cracker

1 marshmallow

Half of a chocolate bar

108

Step 1 Break graham cracker in half.

Let's **Think** About...

How do the captions and photos on page 108 assist you with what you need?
Procedural Text

Step 2 Put the chocolate on one half of the graham cracker. Save the other half for the top.

Step 3 Place the marshmallow on top of the chocolate.

Let's **Think** About...

How do the captions and photos help you follow the steps?
Procedural Text

109

Let's **Think** About...

Why is it important that an adult help you with these steps?

Procedural Text

Step 4 Put it on a plate, and have an adult heat it in the microwave on HIGH for 10–15 seconds.

Step 5 When done, have the adult take it out of the microwave, and let it cool for a few seconds.

Step 6 Press the other half of the graham cracker on top of the marshmallow.

Step 7 Let it cool further, and enjoy it like it was made over the campfire!

Let's **Think** About...

Reading Across Texts *Henry and Mudge and the Starry Night* and "How to Make a S'more" show fun things to do. Do you think Henry and his family would make s'mores while camping?

Writing Across Texts Write a list of things you would like to do on a camping trip.

111

Common Core State Standards
Foundational Skills 4.b. Read on-level text orally with accuracy, appropriate rate, and expression on successive readings.
Also Speaking/Listening 1., Language 5.

Let's
Learn
It!

READING STREET ONLINE
VOCABULARY ACTIVITIES
www.ReadingStreet.com

Vocabulary

A **synonym** is a word that has the same or almost the same meaning as another word.

big

large

Big is a synonym of *large*.

Practice It! Write each word and identify its synonym. Then write sentences using the synonyms.

1. start   **2.** little

3. fluffy   **4.** toss

Media Literacy

Get Ready For Grade 3

Notice how media can inform or entertain.

Recognize Different Purposes of Media

The media is a way to communicate with many people all at once. Media can give facts or news. It can entertain us. Newspapers and the Internet are media. Television is a media too.

Practice It! Name a media. Think of a fact you learned from it. Tell your class about it. Be sure to speak clearly. Then share with the class a media by which you were entertained and why.

Fluency

Read with Accuracy and Appropriate Rate

Read all the words. Do not leave any words out. Read as though you are speaking. Do not read too fast or too slow. Then you will understand what you read.

Practice It!

1. She likes to camp.

2. The hiker saw animal tracks on the path.

3. The bears sleep inside a big cave.

Common Core State Standards

Language 6. Use words and phrases acquired through conversations, reading and being read to, and responding to texts, including using adjectives and adverbs to describe (e.g., *When other kids are happy that makes me happy*). **Also Speaking/Listening 1.**

Oral Vocabulary

Let's Talk About

Exploring the Desert

- Share information about exploring the desert.

- Share ideas about what is found in the desert.

READING STREET ONLINE
CONCEPT TALK VIDEO
www.ReadingStreet.com

Common Core State Standards
Spiral Review Foundational Skills 2.
Demonstrate understanding of spoken
words, syllables, and sounds (phonemes).

Phonemic Awareness

Let's Listen for

Sounds

- Find the turtle. Say a word that tells what it does.

- Say a word that tells what the tarantula is doing. Now say each sound in the word.

- Say a word that tells what the roadrunners have done. Now say each sound in the word.

READING STREET ONLINE
SOUND-SPELLING CARDS
www.ReadingStreet.com

116

117

Common Core State Standards
Foundational Skills 3. Know and apply grade-level phonics and word analysis skills in decoding words.
Also Foundational Skills 3.f.

Envision It! | Sounds to Know

drinking

-ing

pulls

-s

filled

-ed

twisted

-ed

READING STREET ONLINE
SOUND-SPELLING CARDS
www.ReadingStreet.com

Phonics

🎯 Inflected Endings

Words I Can Blend

s t o p p i n g

t r a d e d

p e n s

t e l l i n g

h a p p e n e d

Sentences I Can Read

1. Is Will stopping at his home?

2. Jan traded pens with Steve.

3. Mom is telling Dad what happened.

I Can Read!

Kids like spotting wild animals. Kids can set eyes on snakes, rabbits, and foxes early and late in the day. It is fun spotting them. Jen likes gazing at animals. Where has she tracked them? Animals like water. They will rest at ponds and lakes if it is not too warm. These places can be full of animals. Jen has gazed at rabbits close to a big pond. She takes notes, naming things she spots.

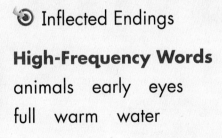

You've learned

⊙ Inflected Endings

High-Frequency Words
animals   early   eyes
full   warm   water

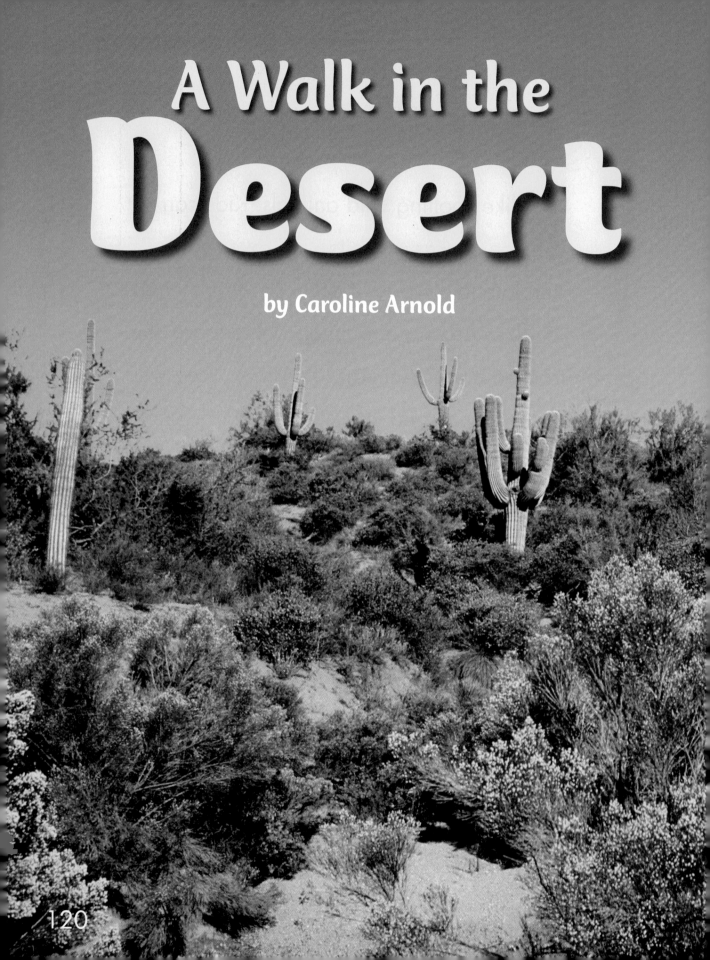

A Walk in the Desert

by Caroline Arnold

Genre

Expository text tells facts about a topic. In the next selection, you will read about a walk in the desert.

Question of the Week
What can we learn by exploring the desert?

See the bright sun. Feel the dry air. It is hot—very hot! Where are we?

We're in the desert. Let's take a walk and see what we can find.

The ground is dry in the desert. It almost never rains. With so little water, it is hard for anything to live. But many plants and animals make their home in this harsh climate. You just have to look closely to see them.

Hedgehog cactus

Teddy-bear cholla cactus

Cactus is one kind of plant that grows in the desert. It doesn't have leaves. Instead, it has sharp spines. The spines protect the cactus from animals who might want to eat it. A cactus stores water in its stem. It uses the water when there is no rain.

Prickly pear cactus

Barrel cactus

Saguaro cactus

Look up at the tall saguaro. It is a giant among cactus plants. It took many years to grow so tall.

In late spring, white flowers bloom. Birds and insects drink the flowers' sweet nectar. After the flowers die, a red fruit grows.

Prickly pear fruit

Saguaro cactus with white flowers

Hawk

The saguaro cactus is home to many desert creatures. *Tap, tap, tap,* pecks a woodpecker. It is carving a hole for its nest. Old holes become nests for other birds.

A hawk is searching for food below. Its sharp eyes can spot even a tiny mouse.

Woodpecker

Owl

What is that large bird? It's a roadrunner. *Coo, coo, coo,* it calls. The roadrunner hardly ever flies, but it can run fast. Watch it chase a lizard to eat.

Roadrunner

Tree lizard

Here are some other lizards.
Lizards need the sun's heat to
warm their scaly bodies. But
when it gets too hot, they look
for shade.

Zebra-tailed lizard

Leopard lizard

Short-horned lizard

A rattlesnake lies next to a rock. Its earth colors make it hard to see. Rattlesnakes are dangerous. A bite from one will kill a small animal. If you hear a rattlesnake shake its tail, it is trying to scare you away.

Look! Did you see that rock move? It isn't a rock at all. It's a desert tortoise. The hard shell protects the tortoise from enemies and from the hot sun. The tortoise uses its sharp beak to break off tough desert grasses. It sometimes eats cactus fruits, too.

Rattlesnake

Cactus fruits

Desert tortoise

The jack rabbit is also a plant eater. Watch it sniff the early evening air. It is alert to the sounds and smells of the desert. When danger is near, the jack rabbit's long legs help it to escape quickly.

Jack rabbits

As night begins to fall, the desert air cools. Animals who were hidden or sleeping come out to hunt and feed. A hungry coyote howls to the moon.

Do you see the small kit fox? Big ears help the fox to hear well so it can track animals to eat.

The cool night is full of activity.

Kangaroo rat

Small kit fox

Owl

Coyote

135

The desert is an exciting place to visit. You can ride a mule along a deep canyon, slide down a sand dune, learn about wildlife at a nature center, or taste sweet jelly made from prickly pear fruit.

Prickly pear fruit

Riding a mule

Sliding down a sand dune

137

You can find deserts all over the world. Not all deserts are alike. Some are hot. Others are cold. But in all deserts there is little rain.

North America

The deserts in South America have very little animal or plant life.

South America

The Gila monster is the only poisonous lizard in the American Desert.

The Gobi Desert is cold and snowy in the winter. Temperatures are often below freezing.

The tiny fennec fox lives in the world's largest desert—the Sahara.

Asia

Europe

Africa

The Australian Desert is home to the bandicoot.

Australia

The dromedary is a one-humped camel found in the sandy Arabian Desert.

Can you find the continent where you live?

Is there a desert on it?

139

Common Core State Standards
Informational Text 1. Ask and answer such questions as *who, what, where, when, why,* and *how* to demonstrate understanding of key details in a text. **Also Informational Text 2.**

Envision It! | Retell

READING STREET ONLINE
STORY SORT
www.ReadingStreet.com

Think Critically

1. How is a desert like a forest? How is it different? Text to World

2. Why do you think the author took us on a "walk" through the desert? Author's Purpose

3. What is the main idea of the text? Look back and distinguish the main idea from the topic.

  Main Idea and Details

4. Locate facts and details about the saguaro cactus and desert animals on pages 125–126. How do the pictures help?

  Important Ideas

5. Look Back and Write Look back at page 133. How does a jack rabbit protect itself? Provide evidence to support your answer.

Key Ideas and Details • Text Evidence

Caroline Arnold

Caroline Arnold has walked in several deserts in the southwestern United States. After she moved to California, she says, "I grew to love the desert."

Ms. Arnold is fascinated by the way living things adapt to the extreme heat and cold and the lack of water in the desert. "I get a thrill out of watching birds, squirrels, rabbits, coyotes, peccaries, lizards, and other desert animals when I spend time in the desert," she says.

Here are other books by Caroline Arnold.

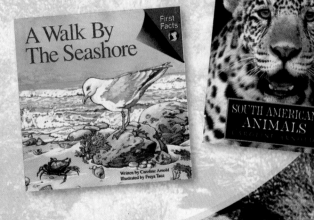

Use the Reading Log in the *Reader's and Writer's Notebook* to record your independent reading.

141

Common Core State Standards

Writing 2. Write informative/explanatory texts in which they introduce a topic, use facts and definitions to develop points, and provide a concluding statement or section. **Also Language 1.e., 1.f.**

Let's Write It!

Key Features of a Brief Report

- is a short informational article

- gives facts and details about a real-life topic

- presents information in an organized way

READING STREET ONLINE
GRAMMAR JAMMER
www.ReadingStreet.com

Brief Report

A **brief report** is a short informational article. It uses facts and details. The student model on the next page is an example of a brief report.

Writing Prompt Think about your neighborhood. Now write a report about who and what live there.

Writer's Checklist

Remember, you should . . .

☑ organize information about your topic.

☑ include facts and details in your report.

☑ use descriptive words.

☑ use declarative and interrogative sentences.

My Neighborhood

My neighborhood has a big park and our red-brick school, North School. People, animals, and plants live around here.

The park has [tall and beautiful trees.] What else lives in my neighborhood? Squirrels live here and collect nuts. People walk on paths. There is a soccer field. Kids play there after school.

Genre
A **report** includes facts.

Writing Trait Word Choice
The writer uses vivid descriptive words.

The writer includes an **interrogative sentence.**

Conventions

Kinds of Sentences

Remember **Declarative sentences** end with periods. An **interrogative sentence** ends with a question mark (**?**).

Common Core State Standards
Informational Text 5. Know and use various text features (e.g., captions, bold print, subheadings, glossaries, indexes, electronic menus, icons) to locate key facts or information in a text quickly and efficiently. **Also Informational Text 6.**

21st Century Skills
INTERNET GUY

Can you trust what you read on the Internet? You should always find out who wrote what you read. Can you believe that person? How can you tell? It is important to always check.

- You can find information quickly using online reference sources.

- Online reference sources may have links to Web sites that will have more information.

- Web sites that end with *.gov* or *.edu* usually have good information.

- Read "Rain Forests." Use the text and pictures to learn about online reference sources.

Rain Forests

Sammy read *A Walk in the Desert* and learned a lot. However, he knows that deserts are not everywhere. In fact, his home is near a forest. His family often goes there to fish, swim, and picnic. *But what exactly is a forest?* Sammy asks himself. To find out more, he goes to an online reference Web site.

Here Sammy finds four different sources: an atlas, an almanac, a dictionary, and an encyclopedia. Sammy clicks on Encyclopedia. Then he types the keyword *forest* into the search engine and clicks on "Go." He gets a list of results that begins like this:

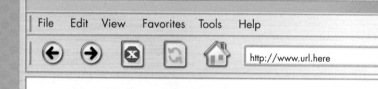

File   Edit   View   Favorites   Tools   Help

http://www.url.here

Search Results: forest

forest (encyclopedia)
forest, a dense growth of trees, together with other plants, covering a large area of land

Sammy clicks on the *forest* link and finds an encyclopedia article. As he reads it, he finds a link to Types of Forests. This makes him curious. He clicks on Types of Forests and finds this information.

File   Edit   View   Favorites   Tools   Help

http://www

Types of Forests

You can find rain forests all over the world, including Central and South America and Central and West Africa. Parts of Asia and Australia also have rain forests. Rain forests get lots of rain every year—from 160 to 400 inches. The average temperature is 80°F. Many different kinds of plants and animals live in rain forests.

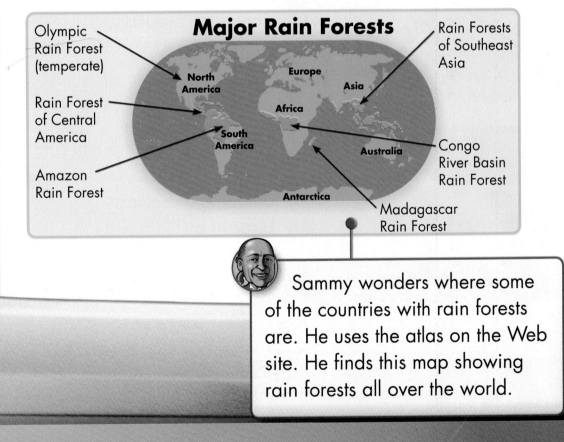

Major Rain Forests

Olympic Rain Forest (temperate)

Rain Forest of Central America

Amazon Rain Forest

North America

Europe

Asia

Africa

South America

Australia

Antarctica

Rain Forests of Southeast Asia

Congo River Basin Rain Forest

Madagascar Rain Forest

Sammy wonders where some of the countries with rain forests are. He uses the atlas on the Web site. He finds this map showing rain forests all over the world.

So far, Sammy has read part of an encyclopedia article and looked at a map. Sammy now goes back to the online reference Web site. He wants to find pictures of animals that live in rain forests. Sammy follows the steps and does another search. He finds these pictures on the Web site of a large university.

http://www.url.here

Trees are the foundation of the rain forest. This tree is *Pterocarpus*. Its roots grow above the ground.

Toucans live in South and Central America. Toucans are among the prettiest birds in a rain forest.

Some crocodiles grow to a very large size—up to twenty feet. But smaller ones (ten feet) are more usual.

Some native South Americans use the poison from poison dart frogs to make darts for hunting.

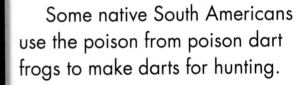

Sammy is so interested that he continues searching until he finds out all he needs to know about rain forests.

Common Core State Standards
Speaking/Listening 4. Tell a story or recount an experience with appropriate facts and relevant, descriptive details, speaking audibly in coherent sentences.
Also Foundational Skills 4.

Let's **Learn** It!

READING STREET ONLINE
VOCABULARY ACTIVITIES
www.ReadingStreet.com

Vocabulary

To **alphabetize** words, put them in order of the letters in the alphabet. Alphabetize by the first letter. If two words begin with the same letter, look at the second letter.

Practice It! Read these words. Write them in alphabetical order by second letter.

dune   desert   dry   do

Fluency

Read with Appropriate Phrasing When reading, stop for a short time when you see a question mark or period. Then start reading again.

Practice It!

1. Who painted that picture? I painted this one.

2. Do you like to camp? I like to camp.

148

Narrate in Sequence

To retell a story, tell what happened to the characters in order. Tell what happened in the beginning, middle, and end. Speak clearly. Do not talk too fast.

Practice It! Retell the story *Henry and Mudge and the Starry Night*. Tell what happened in the beginning, middle, and end of the story. Look at the pictures to help you as you retell the story. Take turns speaking.

Tips

Listening ...

- Listen carefully as others speak.

Speaking ...

- Make eye contact when you speak.

Teamwork ...

- Only speak when it's your turn.

Common Core State Standards

Language 6. Use words and phrases acquired through conversations, reading and being read to, and responding to texts, including using adjectives and adverbs to describe (e.g., *When other kids are happy that makes me happy*).
Also Speaking/Listening 1.

Oral Vocabulary

Let's Talk About

Exploring for Answers

- Share information about exploring new places.

- Share ideas about asking others for help.

READING STREET ONLINE
CONCEPT TALK VIDEO
www.ReadingStreet.com

Phonemic Awareness

Let's Listen for

Sounds

- Find three things that have the sound /ch/. Say each word.

- Find something that begins with the sound /th/. Say each sound in the word.

- Find something that begins with the sound /sh/. Say each sound in the word.

**READING STREET ONLINE
SOUND-SPELLING CARDS
www.ReadingStreet.com**

152

Envision It! | Sounds to Know

chair

ch

watch

shark

tch

feather

sh

whale

th

wh

Phonics

Consonant Digraphs
ch, tch, sh, th, wh

Words I Can Blend

c a tch

f i sh

ch o s e

p a th

th r i l l e d

wh i t e

Sentences I Can Read

1. Brad can catch fish at Duck
Lake.

2. Kate chose that path.

3. Rich is thrilled with his new
white bike.

154

I Can Read!

Chad and Josh often ride to the ranch together. Even though these kids like riding bikes, that path to the ranch has bumps and rocks. The ranch has a pond with fish. Chad and Josh can catch fish using pieces of pancakes. While fishing, these kids check out planes up above. When those planes have gone, Chad and Josh check which plants on the ranch they can name. At that ranch, these kids can learn about lots of stuff. They are thrilled. It is a very nice time.

You've learned

🔵 Consonant Digraphs *ch, tch, sh, th, wh*

High-Frequency Words
gone   learn   often   pieces
though   together   very

The Strongest One

retold as a play by Joseph Bruchac
from *Pushing Up the Sky*
illustrated by David Diaz

Drama is a story written to be acted out for others. Next you will read a drama about an ant who sets out to learn who is the strongest one.

Question of the Week

How does exploration help us find answers?

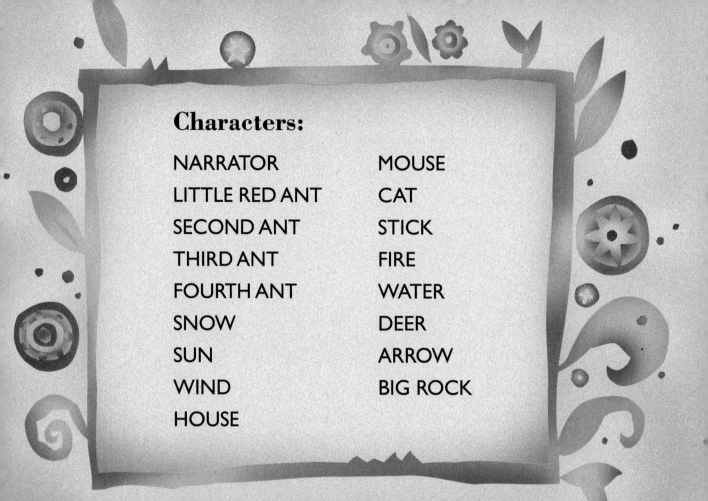

Characters:

NARRATOR	MOUSE
LITTLE RED ANT	CAT
SECOND ANT	STICK
THIRD ANT	FIRE
FOURTH ANT	WATER
SNOW	DEER
SUN	ARROW
WIND	BIG ROCK
HOUSE	

Scene I: Inside the Ant's Hole

(On a darkened stage, the ants crouch together.)

NARRATOR: Little Red Ant lived in a hole under the Big Rock with all of its relatives. It often wondered about the world outside: Who in the world was the strongest one of all? One day in late spring Little Red Ant decided to find out.

LITTLE RED ANT: I am going to find out who is strongest. I am going to go outside and walk around.

SECOND ANT: Be careful! We ants are very small. Something might step on you.

THIRD ANT: Yes, we are the smallest and weakest ones of all.

FOURTH ANT: Be careful, it is dangerous out there!

LITTLE RED ANT: I will be careful. I will find out who is strongest. Maybe the strongest one can teach us how to be stronger.

Scene II: The Mesa

(Ant walks back and forth onstage.)

NARRATOR: So Little Red Ant went outside and began to walk around. But as Little Red Ant walked, the snow began to fall.

(Snow walks onstage.)

LITTLE RED ANT: Ah, my feet are cold. This snow makes everything freeze. Snow must be the strongest. I will ask. Snow, are you the strongest of all?

SNOW: No, I am not the strongest.

LITTLE RED ANT: Who is stronger than you?

SNOW: Sun is stronger. When Sun shines on me, I melt away. Here it comes!

(As Sun walks onstage, Snow hurries offstage.)

LITTLE RED ANT: Ah, Sun must be the strongest. I will ask. Sun, are you the strongest of all?

SUN: No, I am not the strongest.

LITTLE RED ANT: Who is stronger than you?

SUN: Wind is stronger. Wind blows the clouds across the sky and covers my face. Here it comes!

(As Wind comes onstage, Sun hurries offstage with face covered in hands.)

LITTLE RED ANT: Wind must be the strongest. I will ask. Wind, are you the strongest of all?

WIND: No, I am not the strongest.

LITTLE RED ANT: Who is stronger than you?

WIND: House is stronger. When I come to House, I cannot move it. I must go elsewhere. Here it comes!

(As House walks onstage, Wind hurries offstage.)

LITTLE RED ANT: House must be the strongest. I will ask. House, are you the strongest of all?

HOUSE: No, I am not the strongest.

LITTLE RED ANT: Who is stronger than you?

HOUSE: Mouse is stronger. Mouse comes and gnaws holes in me. Here it comes!

(As Mouse walks onstage, House hurries offstage.)

163

LITTLE RED ANT: Mouse must be the strongest. I will ask. Mouse, are you the strongest of all?

MOUSE: No, I am not the strongest.

LITTLE RED ANT: Who is stronger than you?

MOUSE: Cat is stronger. Cat chases me, and if Cat catches me, Cat will eat me. Here it comes!

(As Cat walks onstage, Mouse hurries offstage, squeaking.)

LITTLE RED ANT: Cat must be the strongest. I will ask. Cat, are you the strongest of all?

CAT: No, I am not the strongest.

LITTLE RED ANT: Who is stronger than you?

CAT: Stick is stronger. When Stick hits me,
I run away. Here it comes!

*(As Stick walks onstage, Cat hurries
offstage, meowing.)*

LITTLE RED ANT: Stick must be the strongest.
I will ask. Stick, are you the strongest of all?

STICK: No, I am not the strongest.

LITTLE RED ANT: Who is stronger than you?

STICK: Fire is stronger. When I am put into Fire,
Fire burns me up! Here it comes!

(As Fire walks onstage, Stick hurries offstage.)

LITTLE RED ANT: Fire must be the strongest. I will ask. Fire, are you the strongest of all?

FIRE: No, I am not the strongest.

LITTLE RED ANT: Who is stronger than you?

FIRE: Water is stronger. When Water is poured on me, it kills me. Here it comes!

(As Water walks onstage, Fire hurries offstage.)

LITTLE RED ANT: Water must be the strongest. I will ask. Water, are you the strongest of all?

WATER: No, I am not the strongest.

LITTLE RED ANT: Who is stronger than you?

WATER: Deer is stronger. When Deer comes, Deer drinks me. Here it comes!

(As Deer walks onstage, Water hurries offstage.)

LITTLE RED ANT: Deer must be the strongest. I will ask. Deer, are you the strongest of all?

DEER: No, I am not the strongest.

LITTLE RED ANT: Who is stronger than you?

DEER: Arrow is stronger. When Arrow strikes me, it can kill me. Here it comes!

(As Arrow walks onstage, Deer runs offstage with leaping bounds.)

LITTLE RED ANT: Arrow must be the strongest. I will ask. Arrow, are you the strongest of all?

ARROW: No, I am not the strongest.

LITTLE RED ANT: Who is stronger than you?

ARROW: Big Rock is stronger. When I am shot from the bow and I hit Big Rock, Big Rock breaks me.

LITTLE RED ANT: Do you mean the same Big Rock where the Red Ants live?

ARROW: Yes, that is Big Rock. Here it comes!

(As Big Rock walks onstage, Arrow runs offstage.)

LITTLE RED ANT: Big Rock must be the strongest. I will ask. Big Rock, are you the strongest of all?

BIG ROCK: No, I am not the strongest.

LITTLE RED ANT: Who is stronger than you?

BIG ROCK: You are stronger. Every day you and the other Red Ants come and carry little pieces of me away. Someday I will be gone.

Scene III: The Ant's Hole

NARRATOR: So Little Red Ant went back home and spoke to the ant people.

(The ants crouch together on the darkened stage.)

SECOND ANT: Little Red Ant has returned.

THIRD ANT: He has come back alive!

FOURTH ANT: Tell us about what you have learned. Who is the strongest of all?

LITTLE RED ANT: I have learned that everything is stronger than something else. And even though we ants are small, in some ways we are the strongest of all.

Common Core State Standards

Literature 1. Ask and answer such questions as *who, what, where, when, why,* and *how* to demonstrate understanding of key details in a text.
Also Literature 7., Writing 3.

Envision It! | Retell

Think Critically

1. How are the animals in this story different from those in the selection *A Walk in the Desert*? Text to Text

2. Why do you think the author wrote this story as a play? Author's Purpose

3. What facts does Little Red Ant learn about Fire and Water? Facts and Details

4. How does the picture on page 165 help you predict what is stronger than Stick? Reread to confirm. Predict and Set Purpose

5. **Look Back and Write**
Look back at how the author wrote the play. Identify the elements of dialogue. Use them to write a short play about Little Red Ant and a new character.

Key Ideas and Details • Text Evidence

Joseph Bruchac

As a child, Joseph Bruchac loved to explore nature—the animals, birds, insects, and plants around him. His grandfather, an Abenaki Indian, taught him many things about nature.

Here are other books by Joseph Bruchac.

Today, Mr. Bruchac tells traditional Native American stories. "In the Abenaki Indian tradition," he says, "there is a story connected to just about every bird, animal, and plant." One message in many of these tales is that all parts of nature are important. Even tiny ants can make a difference!

Use the Reading Log in the *Reader's and Writer's Notebook* to record your independent reading.

Common Core State Standards
Writing 3. Write narratives in which they recount a well-elaborated event or short sequence of events, include details to describe actions, thoughts, and feelings, use temporal words to signal event order, and provide a sense of closure. **Also Language 1., 1.f.**

Let's Write It!

Key Features of a Play Scene

- is part of a story that is acted out
- has characters who speak
- character's name at beginning of each speech tells who says it

READING STREET ONLINE
GRAMMAR JAMMER
www.ReadingStreet.com

Narrative

Play Scene

A **play scene** is part of a play, a story that is acted out. The student model on the next page is an example of a play scene.

Writing Prompt Think about the questions Little Red Ant asks the characters in the play. Now write a play scene in which the ant asks another animal or a girl or boy about strength.

Writer's Checklist

Remember, you should . . .

☑ write each character's name before the words the character says.

☑ use at least one imperative sentence and one exclamatory sentence.

176

The Lion's Strength

Little Red Ant: Lion, do you have a strong roar?

Lion: It is true. My roar is strong.

Little Red Ant: Roar so I can hear.

Lion: Roar!

Little Red Ant: Wow, that was really loud! Are you the strongest of all?

Lion: Thorn is stronger than me. When I get Thorn in my paw, I can't walk.

Genre
In a **play scene**, the characters act out the story.

Writing Trait Conventions
Writer capitalizes the names of characters.

An **imperative sentence** ends in a period.

Conventions

Kinds of Sentences

Remember Most **imperative** sentences end with periods. **Exclamatory** sentences end with exclamation marks (**!**).

Common Core State Standards
Informational Text 5. Know and use various text features (e.g., captions, bold print, subheadings, glossaries, indexes, electronic menus, icons) to locate key facts or information in a text quickly and efficiently. **Also Informational Text 2.**

Science in Reading

Genre
Expository Text

- Expository text explains an animal, place, object, or idea.

- Expository text gives facts and details.

- Expository text often has text features, such as headings, and graphic features such as pictures and maps.

- Read "Anteaters." Notice how the headings help you find information.

ANTEATERS
by John Jacobs

Have you ever heard of an anteater? Have you ever seen one? Let's learn more about them.

Central America

South America

Where do they live?

Anteaters live mostly in South and Central America where there are lots of grasses, swamps, and rain forests. These are the kinds of places where many ants live. Anteaters explore these grasses, swamps, and rain forests all day looking for ants to eat.

Let's Think About...

Read the headings in the selection. Which page would you read to learn what anteaters look like? **Expository Text**

Let's Think About...

What is the most important idea about the topic of anteaters on this page? What details support this idea? **Expository Text**

179

What do they look like?

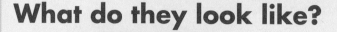

The giant anteater, which is the most common, looks like nothing you've ever seen before. It has a bushy tail and a fat body. It has a tiny mouth, small eyes, and small ears. Its most important body parts are its sharp claws and its long, long tongue. (Its tongue is almost two feet long. That's as long as two rulers put together!)

Let's **Think** About...

What are an anteater's most important body parts?
Expository Text

How do they eat?

An anteater looks for ants by smelling the ground. When it finds an ants' nest, the anteater breaks it open with its sharp claws. It puts its long tongue down into the nest. Ants stick to the tongue and the anteater swallows them. The anteater does this over and over very fast until it is full. The anteater eats only a small number of ants at a time from any one nest. It does not want to run out of food! But ants, beware! It will return.

Let's **Think** About...

Reading Across Texts Would an anteater be a good character to have in the play *The Strongest One*?

Writing Across Texts Write a short paragraph. Tell whether you think an anteater should be in the play. Give a reason for your opinion.

Common Core State Standards
Foundational Skills 4.b. Read on-level text orally with accuracy, appropriate rate, and expression on successive readings.
Also Literature 6., Speaking/Listening 1.a.

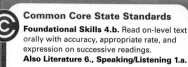

Let's Learn It!

READING STREET ONLINE
VOCABULARY ACTIVITIES
www.ReadingStreet.com

Vocabulary

A **synonym** is a word that has the same or almost the same meaning as another word.

little

small

Practice It! Read these words. Say the synonym for each word, and then write a sentence using it.

hike   leap   look

Fluency

Read with Expression and Intonation When reading aloud, make your voice go up a little at the end of a question. Be sure to understand what you read.

Practice It!

1. Is a tiger bigger than a whale?

2. No, it isn't. Why would you ask?

Listening and Speaking

Speak your lines clearly when giving a play.

Present a Dramatic Interpretation

When you perform a play, you take the part of a character. Try to say your lines the way your character would. Say your lines clearly. Listen as others read their parts.

Practice It! With friends, read lines from *The Strongest One*. Each of you should read the part of one character. Read the words the character says. Do not read the character's name. Speak clearly and at an understandable pace.

Tips

Listening ...

• Listen as others perform.

Speaking ...

• Speak clearly.

Teamwork ...

• Read your lines only when it is your turn.

WORKING
Together

THE BIG
?

How can we
work together?

connect to SOCIAL STUDIES

Common Core State Standards

Language 6. Use words and phrases acquired through conversations, reading and being read to, and responding to texts, including using adjectives and adverbs to describe (e.g., *When other kids are happy that makes me happy*). **Also Speaking/Listening 1.**

Let's Talk About

Dangerous Situations

- Share information about the many dangerous situations in the world.

- Share ideas about the many ways that each of us can help.

READING STREET ONLINE
CONCEPT TALK VIDEO
www.ReadingStreet.com

186

Phonemic Awareness

Let's Listen for

Sounds

- The farmer wants to protect the horses from harm. Change the sound /h/ in *harm* to the sound /f/. Say the new word.

- Find something that rhymes with *far*. Say the sound at the beginning of that word.

- Find two things that rhyme with *born*. Say each sound in those words.

READING STREET ONLINE
SOUND-SPELLING CARDS
www.ReadingStreet.com

188

189

Common Core State Standards
Foundational Skills 3. Know and apply grade-level phonics and word analysis skills in decoding words.
Also Foundational Skills 3.f.

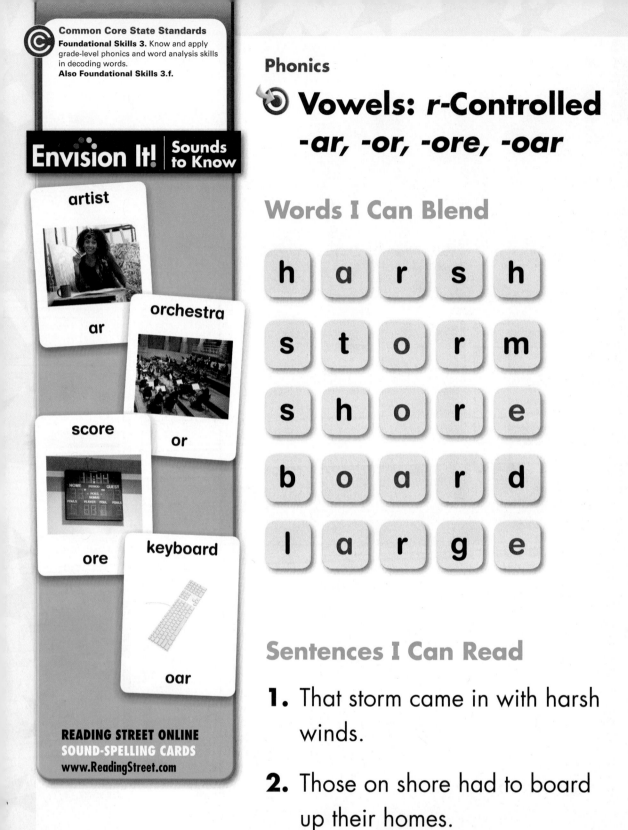

Envision It! | Sounds to Know

artist
ar

orchestra
or

score
ore

keyboard
oar

READING STREET ONLINE
SOUND-SPELLING CARDS
www.ReadingStreet.com

Phonics

🔊 Vowels: *r*-Controlled
-ar, -or, -ore, -oar

Words I Can Blend

h a r s h

s t o r m

s h o r e

b o a r d

l a r g e

Sentences I Can Read

1. That storm came in with harsh winds.

2. Those on shore had to board up their homes.

3. Large ships left the water.

190

I Can Read!

My family does not live far from a water park. It is hard to live close and not play there lots. Mom said, "Listen, we can pull together and finish these chores. Then let us take a break and visit that park." The best part for my brother Jordan is the wave place. He rides on this board as the waves push him back and forth. Once, I heard Jordan yelling my name. I looked and saw him acting like he was in a big storm. A trip to the water park is never boring!

Genre

Literary Nonfiction tells about a true event or a series of events like a story. Now read about two dogs who are fearless friends to their owner.

Tara and Tiree,
Fearless Friends

by Andrew Clements
illustrated by Scott Gustafson

Question of the Week

How can we help each other in dangerous situations?

When Jim was a boy in Canada, his family had dogs. Jim loved those dogs. They were like part of his family.

When Jim grew up, he still loved dogs. He learned how to train them. He helped dogs learn to be good.

He always said, "There is no such thing as a bad dog." Training dogs became Jim's job.

Jim had two dogs named Tara and Tiree.
Tara was mostly black. Tiree was mostly gold.
Jim loved them both, and they loved him too.
Jim and his dogs liked the winter time.

They had good coats to keep warm. They
played in the snow. They went for long walks.

They liked going out, but they liked going back
in too. It was good to sit by the fire and listen to
the wind.

Jim's house was by a lake. Every winter there was ice on it. One day Jim went for a walk out on the lake. Tara and Tiree went too. The dogs loved to run across the ice.

It was very cold. Jim was ready to go back home. Then all at once the ice broke. Jim fell into the cold, cold water.

Jim called for help. No one was near. No one could hear him. But Tara and Tiree heard Jim and came running. Jim wanted the dogs to stay away. He was afraid for them.

But Tiree loved Jim. She wanted to help. When she came near the hole, the ice broke again. Tiree fell into the water with Jim.

The water was so cold. Jim knew he did not have much time. Jim tried to help Tiree get out. But the ice broke more and more.

Jim hoped Tara would run away. He did not want her to fall in the water too. But Tara did not run away. She wanted to help.

First Tara got down low. Then she came closer, little by little. The ice did not break.

Jim put out his hand. Tara got very close. Then Jim got hold of Tara's collar. Jim held on. Tara pulled back, but Jim was too big. He was still in the cold water.

Then Tiree did something very smart. She walked on Jim's back—up and out of the water! Tiree was cold, but she was safe! Did she run off the ice? No. She loved Jim too much to run away.

Tiree got down on her belly like Tara. She got close to Jim. Jim held out his other hand. And he grabbed on to Tiree's collar!

The two dogs pulled back hard. They slipped, but they didn't stop. Slowly they pulled Jim up onto the ice. He was safe.

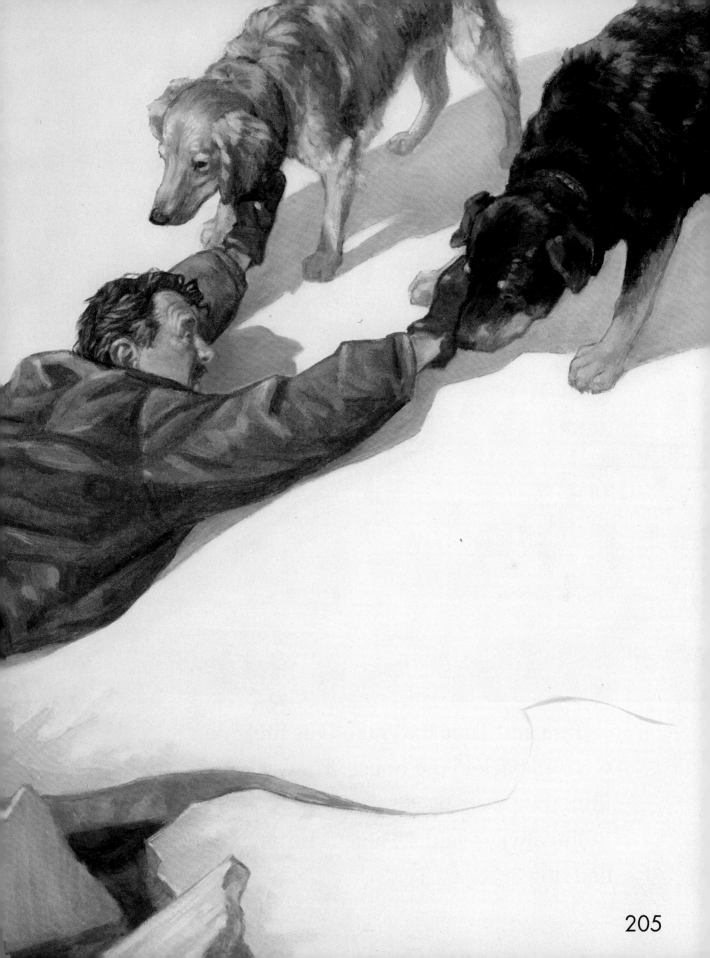

Tara and Tiree had saved his life! Soon they were all back in the house. They sat by the fire until they were warm again.

Jim always said, "There is no such thing as a bad dog."

Now Jim says something else too: "There *is* such a thing as a brave and wonderful dog!"

Jim is sure of this, because he has two of them—Tara and Tiree.

Common Core State Standards
Literature 1. Ask and answer such
questions as *who, what, where, when, why,*
and *how* to demonstrate understanding of
key details in a text.

Envision It! Retell

Think Critically

1. This story is about dogs. What other story did you read about a dog? How are the stories alike? How are they different? Text to Text

2. Why did the author write about rescue dogs? Author's Purpose

3. What happened when Jim tried to lift Tiree out of the water? Cause and Effect

4. Jim says, "There *is* such a thing as a brave and wonderful dog!" Summarize why he feels this way. Summarize

5. Look Back and Write
Look back at page 194. Why does Jim believe that there is no such thing as a bad dog? Provide evidence to support your answer.

Key Ideas and Details • Text Evidence

Meet the Author

Andrew Clements

Andrew Clements says, "Every good writer I know started off as a good reader." When Mr. Clements was growing up, he loved to read. He remembers a school librarian who made him feel he was the "owner" of every book he read. He says, "That's one of the greatest things about reading a book—read it, and you own it forever."

Mr. Clements once taught school. Because he believes books make a difference, he read to his students in the classroom and to his four sons at home.

Here are other books by Andrew Clements.

Use the Reading Log in the *Reader's and Writer's Notebook* to record your independent reading.

209

Common Core State Standards
Writing 3. Write narratives in which they recount a well-elaborated event or short sequence of events, include details to describe actions, thoughts, and feelings, use temporal words to signal event order, and provide a sense of closure. **Also Language 1.**

Let's Write It!

Key Features of Narrative Nonfiction

- tells a story about real people and events
- usually shows events in the order they happened

READING STREET ONLINE
GRAMMAR JAMMER
www.ReadingStreet.com

Narrative Nonfiction

Narrative nonfiction tells about things that really happened. The student model on the next page is an example of narrative nonfiction.

Writing Prompt Think about ways people work together in dangerous situations. Now write a narrative nonfiction paragraph about rescue workers.

Writer's Checklist

Remember, you should . . .

- ✓ tell a short true story about rescue workers.
- ✓ use words to show how you feel about the event.
- ✓ use nouns correctly.

210

Firefighters

There was a fire at a house on my street. We could see tall flames. It was scary. Then we heard sirens. We knew the firefighters were coming. They made sure everyone was safe. Then they got a big hose. They sprayed the house with water and put the fire out. Firefighters are very brave.

Writing Trait Voice The sentence shows how the writer feels.

Genre Narrative nonfiction tells about a real event.

Nouns name persons, places, animals, or things.

Conventions

 Nouns

Remember A **noun** names a person, place, animal, or thing.

 A **boy** saw his **dog** at **home**.

211

Social Studies in Reading

Rescue Dogs

by Rena Moran

Genre
Expository Text

- Expository text explains an object or idea.

- Expository text gives facts.

- Expository text often has text and graphic features, such as headings and pictures.

- Read "Rescue Dogs." Look for elements of expository text in this selection.

Do you know that dogs can be trained to save lives? They are called rescue dogs. When people are in danger, rescue dogs are ready to help them.

Who do they help?

Rescue dogs find people who are lost or trapped. The dogs must be strong and smart. They must listen to the people who train and handle them. This dog's trainer is telling him where to go look for a person who is trapped in snow.

What dogs make good rescue dogs?

Some dogs, like bloodhounds and German shepherds, are good at following the scent trails of lost people. German shepherds are also good at finding people who are trapped under snow.

Newfoundlands are good swimmers. They do a great job with water rescues.

Let's Think About...

Look at the heading on this page. What information do you think this page gives?
Expository Text

How do they do their jobs?

Like all dogs, rescue dogs have a very good sense of smell. They use their sense of smell to find a lost person.

A rescue dog can follow the scent trail a person has left.

Let's **Think** About...

How does a rescue dog follow the trail of a lost person?

Expository Text

Sometimes more than one person is lost. Rescue dogs can look for more than one person at a time.

Rescue dogs could not do their jobs without the people who train and handle them. Most of these people love working with dogs. They also like rescuing people in danger—just like their dogs do!

Let's Think About...

Reading Across Texts "Rescue Dogs" says that rescue dogs must be "strong and smart." Are Tara and Tiree in *Tara and Tiree, Fearless Friends* strong and smart?

Writing Across Texts Write a short paragraph explaining your answer.

Common Core State Standards
Language 4.a. Use sentence-level context as a clue to the meaning of a word or phrase. **Also Foundational Skills 4., Speaking/Listening 2.**

Vocabulary

Look at the words and pictures around the **unfamiliar word** to find the meaning of the word.

Practice It! Decide the relevant meaning of each bold word. Tell what words helped you.

1. The water was **frigid**. I shivered when I put my hand in the icy, cold water.

2. The room was clean and **tidy**. Everything was neat.

Fluency

Accuracy and Appropriate Rate

When you read, read only the words you see. Do not read too fast or too slow. Then you will understand what you are reading.

Practice It! Read the sentences aloud.

1. Did you hear dogs barking?

2. The dogs play with the ball.

Listening and Speaking

Listen carefully when following instructions.

Give and Follow Instructions

Instructions tell how to do something. When giving instructions, tell the steps in order. When listening, ask questions to be sure you understand each step.

Practice It! Tell a friend how to write and then erase your name on the board. Use the correct nouns as you tell each step. Ask your partner to repeat the instructions and to follow them. Take turns.

Tips

Listening ...

- Follow oral instructions in the sequence they are given.

Speaking ...

- Restate oral instructions to make sure you understand.

- Speak clearly when giving oral instructions.

Common Core State Standards

Language 6. Use words and phrases acquired through conversations, reading and being read to, and responding to texts, including using adjectives and adverbs to describe (e.g., *When other kids are happy that makes me happy*).
Also Speaking/Listening 1.

Oral Vocabulary

Let's Talk About

Changing History

- Share information about how working together has changed history.

- Share ideas about how working together has made many positive changes.

READING STREET ONLINE
CONCEPT TALK VIDEO
www.ReadingStreet.com

218

Common Core State Standards
Spiral Review Foundational Skills 2.
Demonstrate understanding of spoken words, syllables, and sounds (phonemes).

Let's Listen for

Sounds

- Use a contraction to describe something in the picture. Say each sound in the contraction.

- Use the contraction *it's* in a sentence about something in the picture. Say each sound in *it's*.

READING STREET ONLINE
SOUND-SPELLING CARDS
www.ReadingStreet.com

Common Core State Standards
Language 2.c. Use an apostrophe to form contractions and frequently occurring possessives.
Also Foundational Skills 3., 3.f.

Envision It! | Sounds to Know

can + not=
can't

contraction

he + is=
he's

contraction

she + will=
she'll

contraction

I + am =
I'm

contraction

Phonics

Contractions

Words I Can Blend

h a v e n 't

i t 's

w e 'l l

I 'm

s h e 's

Sentences I Can Read

1. Haven't Mom and Dad said that it's going to rain?

2. We'll get a ride home.

3. I'm swimming, but she's walking.

I Can Read!

It started as the worst day. Some day I'll laugh about it, but I'm certainly sad today. It started when Dad took me to the bus stop. He had helped me read for a big test. Dad said, "You are set. That test will go well."

The second we got to that stop, our pup, Max, ran down the path. "Great, " Dad said. "Either we left that gate open, or he's jumped it." We got Max. But by then the bus had left, and I had missed my test. I haven't made it up yet. I'll do that at lunch.

You've learned

 Contractions

High-Frequency Words
certainly either great laugh second worst you're

Abraham Lincoln

written by Delores Malone

illustrated by Stephen Costanza

Informational text often gives facts about real people, places, and events that reflect history or the traditions of communities.

Question of the Week

How has working together changed history?

225

It was clean up time in Ms. Grant's second grade class. Noah and Maya were putting away the big map of the United States. Suddenly, there was the worst ripping sound.

Everyone looked at Noah and Maya. The map was torn into two pieces.

"Look what you did!" said Noah.

"Me?" said Maya. "You're wrong! It's not my fault!"

Ms. Grant stepped in. "Please stop," she said. "I don't think either of you is at fault. We can fix that." They held up the two pieces of the map.

"Look! Our country has been torn in two. We need Abraham Lincoln!"

"Abraham Lincoln?" asked Noah. "You mean the President Lincoln from long ago?"

"Yes," said Ms. Grant. "I'll tell you about Abraham Lincoln and how he worked with other people to put our country back together."

Abraham Lincoln was born on February 12, 1809 in Kentucky. His family lived in a log cabin that had only one room. When Abraham Lincoln was a boy, everyone called him "Abe."

Abe and his family moved to Indiana in 1816. He was seven years old. Abe worked very hard on the farm.

One of his jobs was cutting wood. Wood was used for cooking and for heat. Wood was also used to make fences. When Abe grabbed the handle of his ax, a big log soon became firewood or fence rails.

Abe also plowed fields and planted corn. Young Abe carried a book with him wherever he went. Whenever he had time to rest, Abe took the book from his pocket and read.

As a young man, Abe worked in a store in New Salem, Illinois. One day a woman bought some things in the store. After she left, Abe noticed that he hadn't given enough money back to the woman. Abe walked many miles to give her the money. When his friends heard this story, they called him "Honest Abe."

Abe loved to read, tell stories, and make people laugh. Abe studied hard and passed a test to become a lawyer. In 1837, he opened a law office in Springfield, Illinois. Now people called him "Mr. Lincoln."

Abraham Lincoln was elected President of the United States on November 6, 1860. Now he was called "President Lincoln."

President Lincoln had a very big problem. People in the North wanted to end slavery. The people in the South wanted to form their own country and keep slavery. President Lincoln wanted to keep the country together.

1800   1810   1820   1830

1809 Abraham Lincoln is born in Kentucky.

1837 Lincoln opens his law office.

1816 Young Abe and his family move to Indiana.

The Civil War began on April 12, 1861. The armies of the North and the South fought each other. Many people died. President Lincoln had to find a way to stop the fighting.

The Civil War finally ended on April 9, 1865. Abraham Lincoln worked very hard with many others to put our country back together. To this day, many people call Abraham Lincoln "America's Great President."

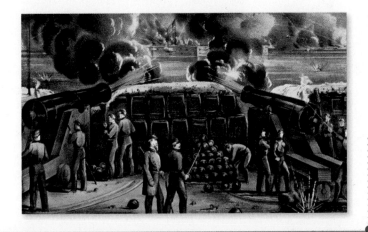

1861 The Civil War begins.

1840   1850   1860   1870

1860 Lincoln is elected President of the United States.

1865 The Civil War ends.

When Ms. Grant finished her story, Maya smiled at Noah and said, "Do you think we could put our country back together again?"

Noah nodded. "We certainly can."

When they finished, Maya and Noah held up the map for the class to see.

"Thank you," said Ms. Grant. "You did a terrific job. Now you have something in common with Abraham Lincoln. You worked together and you put our country back together."

Legend

THE UNITED STATES

Common Core State Standards
Informational Text 1. Ask and answer such questions as *who, what, where, when, why,* and *how* to demonstrate understanding of key details in a text.
Also Informational Text 2.

Envision It! | Retell

240

Think Critically

1. Name U.S. Presidents other than Abraham Lincoln. Text to World

2. Why do you think the author wrote this article—to inform, entertain, or persuade? Explain your answer. Author's Purpose

3. What is the topic of the text? Why does the author want you to know about this topic?

  Author's Purpose

4. How does the story change after page 229? Text Structure

5. Look Back and Write
Look back at page 237. Why do you think people call Abraham Lincoln "America's Great President"? Provide evidence to support your answer.

Key Ideas and Details • Text Evidence

About the Author and the Illustrator

Delores Malone

Delores Malone has worked with small children most of her life. She now teaches others the best ways to work with young people. Ms. Malone lives in Evanston, Illinois, with her husband, Roy.

Stephen Costanza

Stephen Costanza studied music before he studied art. He still loves music, but his chosen career is an illustrator. You can see his illustrations in books, magazines, and advertising, as well as textbooks.

Mr. Costanza lives on the coast of Maine where he enjoys the outdoors.

Here are other books by Stephen Costanza.

Use the Reading Log in the *Reader's and Writer's Notebook* to record your independent reading.

Common Core State Standards

Writing 2. Write informative/explanatory texts in which they introduce a topic, use facts and definitions to develop points, and provide a concluding statement or section. **Also Language 2., 2.a.**

Let's Write It!

Key Features of a Biography

- tells about a real person's life
- tells important facts about the person

READING STREET ONLINE
GRAMMAR JAMMER
www.ReadingStreet.com

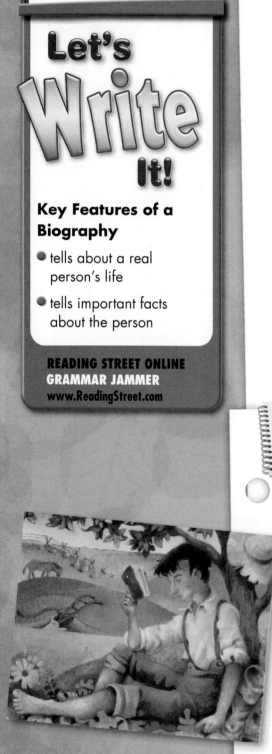

Expository

Biography

A **biography** tells about the life of a real person. The student model on the next page is an example of a short biography.

Writing Prompt Think about someone else in history who worked with others for change. Now write a short biography of that person.

Writer's Checklist

Remember, you should . . .

☑ write about a real person.

☑ focus on important facts and ideas.

☑ capitalize proper nouns, the names of people, places, days, or months.

242

Martin Luther King Jr.

Martin Luther King Jr. spoke out for peace. He worked with others for change. He was an American leader. He helped people get their rights.

Dr. King gave a famous speech. He said that he had a dream. His dream was that all people would be treated fairly. Martin Luther King Jr. Day is on a Monday in January.

Writing Trait Focus The writer tells important ideas about the person.

The **proper nouns,** names of a person, day, and month, are capitalized.

Genre A **biography** tells about a real person.

Conventions

Proper Nouns

- **Remember** Begin **proper nouns,** special names of people, places, animals, and things
- including days and months, with capital letters.

Common Core State Standards
Literature 4. Describe how words and phrases (e.g., regular beats, alliteration, rhymes, repeated lines) supply rhythm and meaning in a story, poem, or song.
Also Literature 1., Informational Text 9.

Social Studies in Reading

Genre
Poetry

- Poetry shows lines of words that have rhythm that is often repeated over and over.

- Rhyming poems end with the same sounds.

- A narrative poem is a poem that tells a story.

- Read "Lincoln." Listen for the elements that make this poetry. Be ready to tell about the rhyme and rhythm.

- Poets often use words in ways that are different from their ordinary meaning. Find the words "heart was set" in the poem. Is this the literal, or real, meaning of the words? Or do the words mean something else?

LINCOLN
by Nancy Byrd Turner

There was a boy of other days,
A quiet, awkward, earnest lad,
Who trudged long weary miles to get
A book on which his heart was set—
And then no candle had!

He was too poor to buy a lamp
But very wise in woodmen's ways.
He gathered seasoned bough and stem,
And crisping leaf, and kindled them
Into a ruddy blaze.

Then as he lay full length and read,
The firelight flickered on his face,
And etched his shadow on the gloom.
And made a picture in the room,
In that most humble place.

The hard years came, the hard years went,
But, gentle, brave, and strong of will,
He met them all. And when to-day
We see his pictured face, we say,
"There's light upon it still."

Let's Think About...

How do **rhyme** and **rhythm** help you see what the boy does?

Let's Think About...

Reading Across Texts What is the same about how these two selections tell about Abraham Lincoln? What is different?

Writing Across Texts Draw a chart. Write what each selection says about Abraham Lincoln.

245

Common Core State Standards
Speaking/Listening 2. Recount or describe key ideas or details from a text read aloud or information presented orally or through other media. **Also Foundational Skills 4.b., Writing 7., Language 2.e.**

Let's **Learn** It!

READING STREET ONLINE
VOCABULARY ACTIVITIES
www.ReadingStreet.com

Vocabulary

Guide words in a dictionary or glossary can help you find words. They are at the top of a page. They show the first and last word on the page.

Practice It! Decide which of the following words would be on a page with these guide words.

clinic   cloth

**class clip clock clue clump
coat clean cost cape clot**

Fluency

Expression

When you read aloud, pay attention to punctuation. Saying some words with more feelings than others makes reading fun. Be sure you understand the reading.

Practice It! Read pages 227 and 228 aloud. Use your voice to show strong feeling when you read the sentences that end with exclamation marks.

Media Literacy

Read or listen to media carefully. Decide on their purpose.

Recognize and Explain Purposes of Media

Some media resources entertain. Some give information. When you look at media resources, explain their purpose. Be sure to speak clearly so listeners can understand what you say. When listening to others, ask questions to be sure you understand.

Practice It! With your group, find media resources that give information about an American President. You might look at Web sites, newspapers, magazines, audiotapes, and DVDs. Share the resources with the class. Explain how you know the resource gives information. Use proper nouns (names). Take turns.

Tips

Speaking ...

• Speak only when it's your turn.

Teamwork ...

• Participate in class discussions.

247

Common Core State Standards

Language 6. Use words and phrases acquired through conversations, reading and being read to, and responding to texts, including using adjectives and adverbs to describe (e.g., *When other kids are happy that makes me happy*).
Also Speaking/Listening 1.

Oral Vocabulary

About

Meeting People's Needs

- Share information about the many decisions required to meet people's needs.

- Share ideas about the work of many people required to meet people's needs.

READING STREET ONLINE
CONCEPT TALK VIDEO
www.ReadingStreet.com

248

You've learned
0 5 6
Amazing Words
so far this year!

Common Core State Standards
Spiral Review Foundational Skills 2.
Demonstrate understanding of spoken
words, syllables, and sounds (phonemes).

Let's Listen for

Sounds

- Find a boy with a colorful shirt. Change the sound /sh/ in *shirt* to the sound /d/. Say the new word.

- Find the picture of the world. Say the sound at the beginning of the word *world*.

- Find something that begins with the same sound as *world*.

READING STREET ONLINE
SOUND-SPELLING CARDS
www.ReadingStreet.com

250

251

Common Core State Standards
Foundational Skills 3. Know and apply grade-level phonics and word analysis skills in decoding words.
Also Foundational Skills 3.f.

Envision It! | **Sounds to Know**

fern

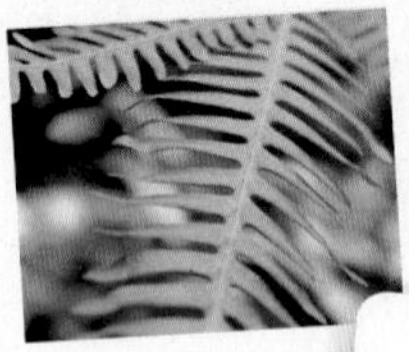

-er

girl

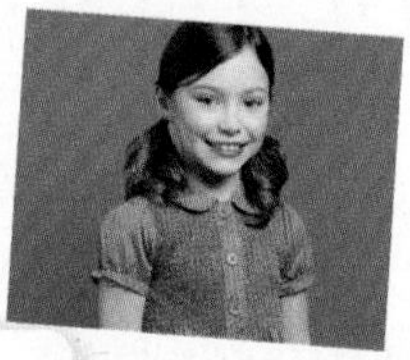

-ir

curtains

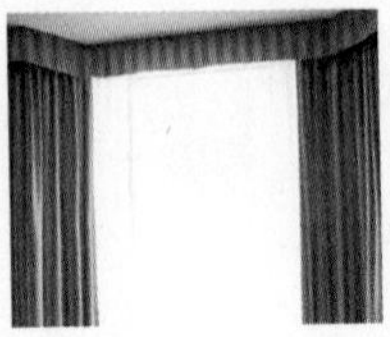

-ur

READING STREET ONLINE
SOUND-SPELLING CARDS
www.ReadingStreet.com

Phonics

Vowels: *r*-Controlled *-er, -ir, -ur*

Words I Can Blend

p e r f e c t

c o r n e r

s q u i r m

h e r

f i r s t

Sentences I Can Read

1. That store is on the perfect corner.

2. Will his pet squirm if it gets bored?

3. This is her first bike.

I Can Read!

A while ago, I spent ten whole days with
my pal Bert and her mom. It was not enough
time! I can tell about Bert in one word—she's
chipper. Above everything, this girl likes fun.
And that girl is not scared to get dirt on her.
Toward the end of that trip, I went with her
family on the water for the first time. Bert
urged me to take a turn with a water board.
I swam instead. This summer it's my turn for
Bert to visit. It will be fun!

You've learned

🔵 Vowels: *r*-Controlled
-er, -ir, -ur

High-Frequency Words
above   ago   enough
toward   whole   word

253

Scarcity

By Janeen R. Adil

Expository text tells facts about a topic. Look for facts that help you understand what *scarcity* means.

Question of the Week

How can we work together to meet people's needs?

What Is Scarcity?

These three girls each want an orange. But only one orange is left. Not all the girls can get what they want.

Things people want and use are resources. Just like these girls, people want more resources than they can have. Sometimes there aren't enough resources for everyone. There is a word for this. It is *scarcity*.

> **Fact!** All countries, rich and poor, have scarcity. No country has enough resources for everything it wants.

How Scarcity Happens

All resources can be scarce. But some resources become more scarce at times. For example, a few years ago, cold weather harmed orange trees.

Then farmers had fewer oranges to pick and sell. Oranges became scarce. There weren't enough oranges for everyone.

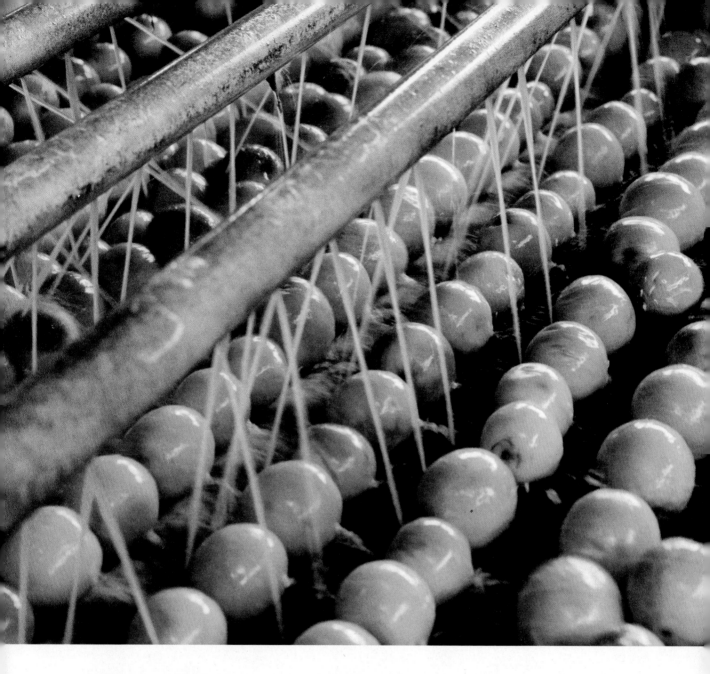

When There Isn't Enough

What happens when oranges are scarce? Then a food company must choose how to use them. The company could make orange juice. Or it could just sell whole, fresh oranges. The company might not be able to do both.

Fact! In 2004, four hurricanes in Florida harmed many fruit trees. Farmers had less fruit to pick and sell during 2005.

Making Trade-Offs

A food company might decide to sell just fresh, whole oranges. That means it's also deciding not to sell juice. The company is making a trade-off. To sell only fresh, whole oranges, it must give something up. The company gives up selling orange juice.

Prices

If oranges are scarce, not everyone can have them. But many people still want to buy oranges.

Stores raise the prices of scarce items. Oranges cost more money when they are scarce. If people want oranges, they must pay a higher price.

Recent severe cold weather in California, Arizona and Mexico has impacted many fruit and vegetable crops.

Many items are now in short supply, which has caused prices to rise.

We apologize for any inconvenience to our customers.

Our Field Buyers, located right in the growing areas, will continue to work diligently to seek out the highest quality fruits and vegetables available.

Minneola Tangelos 99¢

Lemon 5/$1

Texas Oranges 60¢

Red Pears 99¢

Fact! Orange prices were low before the 2004 Florida hurricanes damaged orange trees. After the hurricanes, the prices went up because oranges were scarce.

Making Choices

Scarcity means people have to make choices at the store. If oranges are scarce, what are the choices? People can pay a higher price for oranges. They can also try to find a better price at a different store. Or they can buy another fruit instead.

A Scarce Toy

Just like oranges, toys can be scarce. Ben wants to buy his sister a popular toy for her birthday. But the store near their house has sold out. The toy has become scarce.

Ben Must Choose

Ben looks at other stores around town. At last he finds the toy. But this store is charging a price above what Ben wants to pay.

Now Ben has to make a choice. Should he buy the toy at this high price? Should he keep looking for a better price? Or should he buy his sister something else? What would you do?

Amazing but True!

Cars can't run without gas. In the 1970s, though, there wasn't enough gas. People waited in long lines for hours to fill up their cars. Not everyone who wanted gas could buy it. Some people stopped driving. Toward the end of the shortage, people were turning to walking, riding bikes, or taking the train.

266

Envision It! Retell

READING STREET ONLINE
STORY SORT
www.ReadingStreet.com

Think Critically

1. What would you do if something you wanted to buy was not at the store? Text to Self

2. Why do you think the author wrote this selection—to inform, entertain, or persuade? Explain. Author's Purpose

3. Look back at page 263. How did orange prices change after the 2004 Florida hurricanes? Why? Facts and Details

4. Was something you wanted not at the store? How does this help you understand what scarcity means? Background Knowledge

5. Look Back and Write Look back at pages 260–261. Why isn't the company selling juice? Provide evidence to support your answer.

Key Ideas and Details • Text Evidence

Janeen R. Adil

Janeen R. Adil grew up in a Connecticut farmhouse that is almost 300 years old. In her house, books were everywhere. Her writing grew naturally out of her love of reading.

Ms. Adil especially likes to write nonfiction for young people. She says, "What could be better than showing and sharing the wonders of our world?"

Here are other books by Janeen R. Adil.

Use the Reading Log in the *Reader's and Writer's Notebook* to record your independent reading.

Common Core State Standards
Writing 2. Write informative/explanatory texts in which they introduce a topic, use facts and definitions to develop points, and provide a concluding statement or section. **Also Language 1.**

Let's Write It!

Key Features of Expository Nonfiction

- tells about real people, places, or things
- uses facts and details

READING STREET ONLINE
GRAMMAR JAMMER
www.ReadingStreet.com

Expository Nonfiction

Expository nonfiction

tells facts about a topic. The student model on the next page is an example of expository nonfiction.

Writing Prompt Think about how working together meets the needs of others. Now write an informational paragraph explaining how working together could help someone.

Writer's Checklist

Remember, you should . . .

- ☑ tell about real people, places, or events.
- ☑ choose words that make your meaning clear.
- ☑ use and say singular and plural nouns correctly.

270

Working Together

Our baseball team needed new uniforms. The whole neighborhood helped us raise money. Last Saturday, we had a big rummage sale. Any group can work together to help. We sold old coats, books, and games. We got enough money. Others can work for their goals.

Genre This **expository nonfiction** tells about real people and the effects of work.

Writing Trait Word Choice Exact words, such as *old coats*, make the meaning clear.

These **plural nouns** end in **-s**. Say them, and listen to the sounds at the end.

Conventions

 Singular and Plural Nouns

Remember Singular nouns name one **(book)**. **Plural** nouns name more than one **(books)**. Most plural nouns end in **-s**.

271

Common Core State Standards
Informational Text 5. Know and use various text features (e.g., captions, bold print, subheadings, glossaries, indexes, electronic menus, icons) to locate key facts or information in a text quickly and efficiently.

21st Century Skills
INTERNET GUY

A good site gives you accurate information. How can you tell? Find out who made the site. Can you trust them? A good site is also easy to read. Can you find the information you need?

- A Web site gives information about a topic.

- A Web site may have links to other sites that give more information.

- A Web site may use words and photos to tell about a topic.

- Read "Goods and Services." Use the text and pictures to learn about Web sites and how to see their information.

Goods and Services

After reading *Scarcity*, Jordan wants to learn more about economics. Economics is the science that deals with money, goods, and services. Jordan searches the Web. His parents help him. They find a Web site with many links.

Jordan clicks on one link, Economics. A new Web page opens. He finds these choices:

File   Edit   View   Favorites   Tools   Help

http://www.url.here

Search Results: economics

Goods and Services

Supply and Demand

Needs and Wants

Jordan chooses the link Goods and Services. This link opens to a new Web page.

File   Edit   View   Favorites   Tools   Help

http://www.url.here

Goods and Services

Goods and services are important parts of economics. Goods are things that people use. A good may be something people need to live, like food. A good may also be something people want, just for fun, like a bicycle. Goods can be bought or sold.

Services are things that people do for others. People who provide a service usually do it as part of their jobs. Doctors provide a service by helping people get well. Bus drivers provide a service by taking people to work or to school.

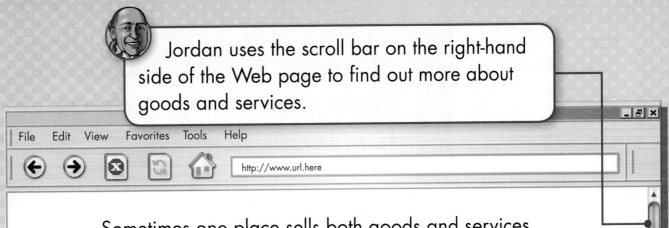

Jordan uses the scroll bar on the right-hand side of the Web page to find out more about goods and services.

File   Edit   View   Favorites   Tools   Help

http://www.url.here

Sometimes one place sells both goods and services. This is a shop where people can buy shampoo and other things for their hair. These are goods. People can also get their hair cut here. The haircuts are a service.

Common Core State Standards
Speaking/Listening 3. Ask and answer questions about what a speaker says in order to clarify comprehension, gather additional information, or deepen understanding of a topic or issue. **Also Foundational Skills 4.**

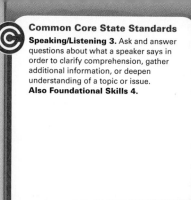

READING STREET ONLINE
VOCABULARY ACTIVITIES
www.ReadingStreet.com

Vocabulary

Time and Order Words for Sequence

Sequence is the order in which things happen. Clue words for sequence can tell the order and time when something happens.

Practice It! Use the clue words below in sentences. Say and write your sentences.

first   last   in
winter   yesterday

Fluency

Appropriate Phrasing Group words as you read. Do not read one word at a time. Be sure you understand what you are reading.

Practice It! Read the sentences aloud. Group the words.

1. Ben and Ted went to the store.

2. At the store, the boys will buy some apples.

Listening and Speaking

Ask and Answer Questions

When you ask a question, look at the person you are asking. Listen politely to the answer. When you answer a question, speak clearly so others can understand you.

Practice It! Take turns asking and answering questions with a friend. Ask what his or her favorite animal is and why. Then ask what his or her favorite color is and why. Use singular and plural nouns.

Tips

Listening . . .

- Listen when someone asks or answers a question.
- Look at the person speaking.

Speaking . . .

- Speak when it is your turn.

Teamwork . . .

- Participate in class activities.

Common Core State Standards

Language 6. Use words and phrases acquired through conversations, reading and being read to, and responding to texts, including using adjectives and adverbs to describe (e.g., *When other kids are happy that makes me happy*).
Also Speaking/Listening 1.

Let's Talk About

Working Together

- Share information about working together to solve problems.

- Share ideas about working together to help get the job done.

READING STREET ONLINE
CONCEPT TALK VIDEO
www.ReadingStreet.com

279

Common Core State Standards
Spiral Review Foundational Skills 2. Demonstrate understanding of spoken words, syllables, and sounds (phonemes).

Phonemic Awareness

Let's Listen for

Sounds

- Find the picture of the foxes. Change the sound /f/ in *foxes* to the sound /b/. Say the new word.

- Find the bunnies in the picture. Say the sound at the beginning of *bunnies*.

- Now find something else that begins with the same sound as *bunnies*.

READING STREET ONLINE
SOUND-SPELLING CARDS
www.ReadingStreet.com

280

281

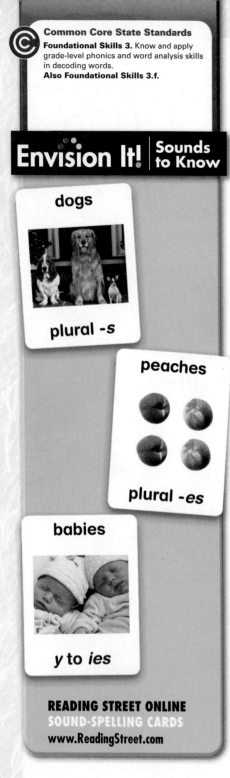

Envision It! | Sounds to Know

dogs

plural -*s*

peaches

plural -*es*

babies

y to *ies*

Phonics

Plurals

Words I Can Blend

s n a k e s

r o c k s

p e n n i e s

h a t s

b u s e s

Sentences I Can Read

1. These snakes came from under those rocks.

2. Can five pennies get me that pencil?

3. Six hats were left on the buses.

I Can Read!

The sign said that the circus will probably pass through our city. "Shall we go and see it?" asked Mom. "We'll sit on benches as the animals pass." Lots of people came for that circus. Kids got out of school. Moms and dads left work. People sat with pet bunnies and puppies. My pals bought snacks for us. We saw circus acts pass homes, stores, and churches. It was a very pleasant time, except my sister Lilly got scared.

You've learned

🎯 Plurals

High-Frequency Words
bought   people   pleasant
probably   scared   shall   sign

The Bremen Town Musicians

retold as a play by Carol Pugliano-Martin
illustrated by Jon Goodell

Drama/Fairy Tale
Drama is a story written to be acted out for others. A **fairy tale** usually takes place long ago and far away and has fantastic characters. Next you will read about four animals that become friends and travel to a faraway town.

Question of the Week

Why is it a good idea to work together?

NARRATOR 1: Once there was a donkey. He worked hard for his owner for many years. Day after day he carried heavy bags of grain to the mill.

NARRATOR 2: But the donkey grew old. He could no longer work hard. One day he heard his owner talking about him. He said he was going to get rid of the donkey. The donkey was worried.

DONKEY: Oh, no! What will happen to me?
I must run away. I'll go to Bremen.
There I can be a fine musician.
(The donkey sings this song:)

Off I go to Bremen Town.
It's the place to be!
I will play my music there.
People will love me!
With a hee-haw here,
And a hee-haw there.
Here a hee, there a haw,
Everywhere a hee-haw.
Off I go to Bremen Town.
It's the place to be!

NARRATOR 1: So the donkey left that night. He had not gone far when he saw a dog lying on the ground.

NARRATOR 2: The dog looked weak. He also looked sad. The donkey knelt down to speak to the dog.

DONKEY: What is the matter, my friend?

DOG: Ah, me. Now that I am old and weak, I can no longer hunt. My owner wants to get rid of me. I got scared, so I ran away. Now I don't know what I will do.

DONKEY: You can come with me to Bremen. I am going to be a musician. Will you join me?

DOG: I'd love to! I can bark very pleasant tunes.

288

DOG AND DONKEY: Off we go to Bremen Town. It's the place to be! We will play our music there. We'll be filled with glee!

DONKEY: With a hee-haw here, and a hee-haw there. Here a hee, there a haw, everywhere a hee-haw.

DOG: With a bow-wow here and a bow-wow there. Here a bow, there a wow, everywhere a bow-wow.

DOG AND DONKEY: Off we go to Bremen Town. It's the place to be!

NARRATOR 1: So, the donkey and the dog set off for Bremen. Soon, they saw a cat sitting by the road.

NARRATOR 2: The cat had the saddest face the donkey and the dog had ever seen. They stopped to find out what was wrong.

DOG: Hello there. Why so glum?

CAT: Ho, hum. Now that I am old and my teeth are not sharp, I cannot catch mice. My owner wants to get rid of me. I don't know what I will do.

DONKEY: You'll come to Bremen with us, that's what! We are going to become musicians. Won't you join us?

CAT: Sure I will! I love to meow.

DONKEY, DOG, AND CAT:

Off we go to Bremen Town.
It's the place to be!
We will play our music there.
We're a gifted three!

DONKEY: With a hee-haw here,
and a hee-haw there.
Here a hee, there a haw,
everywhere a hee-haw.

DOG: With a bow-wow here,
and a bow-wow there.
Here a bow, there a wow,
everywhere a bow-wow.

CAT: With a meow-meow here,
and a meow-meow there.
Here a meow, there a meow,
everywhere a meow-meow.

ALL: Off we go to Bremen Town.
It's the place to be!

NARRATOR 1: The three musicians walked along some more. They came to a farmyard. There they heard a rooster crowing sadly.

ROOSTER: Cock-a-doodle-doo! Cock-a-doodle-doo!

DONKEY: My, you sound so sad. What is wrong?

ROOSTER: I used to crow to wake up the farmer each morning. But he just bought an alarm clock. Now he doesn't need my crowing so he wants to get rid of me. Now I'm a cock-a-doodle-*don't!* Oh, what will I do?

DOG: Come with us to Bremen. We're going to be musicians.

CAT: With your fine crowing, we'll make a wonderful group!

ROOSTER: I *cock-a-doodle-do* think that's a wonderful idea! Let's go!

293

DONKEY, DOG, CAT, AND ROOSTER:

Off we go to Bremen Town. It's the place to be!
We will play our music there. We're a sight to see!

DONKEY: With a hee-haw here, and a hee-haw there.
Here a hee, there a haw, everywhere a hee-haw.

DOG: With a bow-wow here, and a bow-wow there.
Here a bow, there a wow, everywhere a bow-wow.

CAT: With a meow-meow here, and a meow-meow
there. Here a meow, there a meow, everywhere a
meow-meow.

ROOSTER: With a cock-a-doodle here, and a cock-a-doodle there. Here a doodle, there a doodle, everywhere a cock-a-doodle.

ALL: Off we go to Bremen Town. It's the place to be!

NARRATOR 2: The four musicians walked until it got dark. Finally, they saw a sign that said Bremen Town. They danced with excitement, but they were also very tired. They wanted to rest.

NARRATOR 1: They saw light coming from a little house up the road. They walked up to the window, but none of the animals was tall enough to see inside. So, the dog stood on the donkey's back, the cat stood on the dog's back, and the rooster stood on the cat's back and peeked inside.

DOG: What do you see, rooster?

ROOSTER: I think there are three robbers in there! They are sitting at a table full of delicious-looking food!

CAT: Food? I'm starving! What shall we do? We must get them out of that house!

ROOSTER: I have a plan. Listen closely.

NARRATOR 2: The rooster whispered his plan to the others.

296

NARRATOR 1: All of a sudden, the four began singing. They made quite a noise. When the robbers heard the animals, they ran out of the house screaming!

NARRATOR 2: The four musicians went inside the house. There they ate and ate until they were full. Then, it was time for bed.

NARRATOR 1: The donkey slept in the soft grass in the yard. The dog slept behind the front door. The cat slept near the warmth of the fireplace. And the rooster slept high on a bookshelf.

NARRATOR 2: After a while, the robbers returned to finish eating their feast.

ROBBER 1: That noise was probably just the wind. Besides, I can't wait to eat the rest of that roast beef!

ROBBER 2: I can taste those mashed potatoes now!

ROBBER 3: I'll go first just to make sure it's safe.

NARRATOR 1: So the robber went inside. He was cold, so he went to the fireplace to warm himself. There he surprised the cat, who scratched his face.

NARRATOR 2: The robber ran to the front door. The dog was startled and bit his leg. The robber ran outside. He tripped over the donkey, who kicked him.

NARRATOR 1: All this noise woke the rooster up. He started screeching, "Cock-a-doodle-doo!" The robber ran back to his friends.

ROBBER 3: There are four horrible monsters in there! One scratched me with its long nails. Another bit me. Another kicked me. And the fourth one screamed, "Coming to get yooouuuuu!"

ROBBER 1: Four monsters! Let's get out of here!

NARRATOR 2: And the robbers ran off, never to be heard from again.

NARRATOR 1: But the four musicians stayed there. They sang every night in Bremen, where they became the famous Bremen Town Musicians!

Common Core State Standards

Literature 1. Ask and answer such questions as *who, what, where, when, why,* and *how* to demonstrate understanding of key details in a text. **Also Literature 5.**

Envision It! Retell

READING STREET ONLINE
STORY SORT
www.ReadingStreet.com

302

Think Critically

1. How is this play like *The Strongest One?* How is it different? Text to Text

2. Why do you think the author uses narrators in this play? Author's Purpose

3. What happens when the animals sing outside the house on page 297? Cause and Effect

4. What happens first, next, and last in this play? Story Structure

5. Look Back and Write
Look back at the play. How do you know who is speaking? Using the elements of dialogue, write a scene about a fifth Bremen Town Musician.

Key Ideas and Details • Text Evidence

About the Author

Carol Pugliano-Martin

Carol Pugliano-Martin has written many plays for schoolchildren to perform. Some of her plays are about real Americans. Others tell about the heroes of American folk tales. Ms. Pugliano-Martin lives in White Plains, New York.

Here are other books by Carol Pugliano-Martin.

Use the Reading Log in the *Reader's and Writer's Notebook* to record your independent reading.

Common Core State Standards

Writing 3. Write narratives in which they recount a well-elaborated event or short sequence of events, include details to describe actions, thoughts, and feelings, use temporal words to signal event order, and provide a sense of closure. **Also Language 1.b.**

Let's Write It!

Key Features of Fairy Tales

- stories tell about magical characters and events
- characters usually are either very good or very bad

READING STREET ONLINE
GRAMMAR JAMMER
www.ReadingStreet.com

Fairy Tale

A fairy tale has make-believe characters and magical events. *Cinderella* and *Jack and the Beanstalk* are fairy tales. The student model on the next page is an example of a fairy tale.

Writing Prompt Think about a fairy tale in which the characters work together. Now write your own fairy tale about characters who work together.

Writer's Checklist

Remember, you should ...

☑ write a short make-believe story.

☑ write a beginning, middle, and end.

☑ use and say singular and plural nouns correctly.

A New Mouse House

Once a family of good mice lived in the woods. Father and Mother Mouse said, "We need a new home."

Then the mice made a wish. In no time, the walls of a tiny castle were there!

The mice all made a castle out of the walls. The children helped. The mouse family lived happily ever after in the castle.

Genre
Fairy tales tell about magical events.

Some **plural nouns** change spelling. Say *mice*, the plural of *mouse*.

Writing Trait Organization The story has a beginning, middle, and end.

Conventions

Plural Nouns

Remember Plural nouns name more than one. Some plural nouns change spelling. **child**, **children**

305

Common Core State Standards
Literature 2. Recount stories, including fables and folktales from diverse cultures, and determine their central message, lesson, or moral. **Also Literature 1., 4.**

Genre
Folk Tale

- Folk tales are stories that have been handed down over many years.
- Folk tales often have parts repeated.
- Conflicts, or the problems in the story, are often between people or animals that act like people.
- Folk tales often have a moral, or lesson, as a theme.
- Read "A Fool Goes Fishing." Look for elements that make this a folk tale.

A Fool Goes Fishing:
A Retelling of a West African Tale

written by Elizabeth Nielson
illustrated by Dylan Weeks

Near the West African forest, there lived a man named Anansi. Anansi was not good at hunting or fighting or working. He was good at being clever.

One day Anansi invited Anene to go fishing. Anene was quiet and gentle. His friends worried that Anansi would make a fool of him. But Anene was not afraid. "I know all about Anansi," he said.

Anansi and Anene headed for the water. Anene said, "Anansi, let's be partners. I'll cut the branches for the traps, and you can get tired for me."

Anansi didn't like the sound of that. "Absolutely not!" he told Anene. "Why would I want to get tired? I'll cut the branches, and *you* can get tired for *me*!" So Anene sat while Anansi cut the branches.

Let's Think About...

What do we know about Anansi so far? **Folk Tale**

307

Later, it was time to make the traps. Anene said, "Somebody must do the work, and somebody must get tired. Let me do the work."

But Anansi was too clever for Anene. "Certainly not! I'm no fool. I'll be the one to do the work, and you can be the one to get tired." So Anene sat while Anansi made the traps.

Anene tried once more when it was time to put the traps in the water. "There are sharks in this water, Anansi," he said. "I'll wade in with the traps, and you can die for me."

"You expect *me* to die for *you*!" Anansi cried. "You must be a fool! I'll put the traps in the water. If I am bitten, you must die for me!"

Let's Think About...

Why does Anansi do all the work? **Folk Tale**

Let's Think About...

What is the conflict in the story? Who is involved? **Folk Tale**

The next day, Anansi and Anene found a few fish in the traps. Anene said, "Look, Anansi. There will probably be more fish tomorrow. You take these. I'll wait for tomorrow's catch."

"What!" cried Anansi. "You think I'd fall for that! I'll wait for tomorrow's catch. You can have the fish today." So Anene took the fish and sold them at the market.

Each day after that, Anansi was fooled by Anene into waiting for a better catch.

Let's Think About...

How is the conflict building up?
Folk Tale

Let's **Think** About...

How do you think Anansi will respond?
Folk Tale

Finally, the traps rotted. Anene said, "Anansi, it's your turn. I'll take the traps to sell at the market. You can have the last of the fish."

Anansi thought, "I'll bet those traps are worth a lot of money." He told Anene, "No, I'll take the traps. You can have the fish."

But when Anansi tried to sell the traps, the villagers became angry. "Who wants rotten traps?" they cried. "How foolish do you think we are?"

Anansi suddenly didn't feel so clever. He was very tired. He had no money, no fish, and rotten traps. What, he wondered, had gone wrong?

Anene said, "Anansi, remember how you wanted a fool to go fishing with you? Well, the only person you fooled was yourself."

Let's Think About...

What do you think the theme of this story is? Why do you think so?
Folk Tale

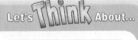

Let's Think About...

Reading Across Texts Both selections use repetition. What parts are repeated in *The Bremen Town Musicians* and "A Fool Goes Fishing"?

Writing Across Texts Write a short paragraph telling why you think the stories use repetition.

311

Common Core State Standards
Literature 6. Distinguish between
characters by speaking in a different voice
for each character when reading aloud.
Also Foundational Skills 4.b.,
Speaking/Listening 1., 1.a.

READING STREET ONLINE
VOCABULARY ACTIVITIES
www.ReadingStreet.com

Vocabulary

A **homophone** is a word that sounds like another word. It has a different spelling and a different meaning.

Practice It! Name the homophones in each sentence. Tell what each homophone means.

1. I write with my right hand.

2. The mouse ate three grapes and eight seeds.

Fluency

Expression

Different characters have different voices. When reading aloud, try to read in the way the character would speak. Be sure to understand what you are reading.

Practice It! Read aloud the sentences with expression.

1. The small spider cries, "Help! I have to hide!"

2. The boy asks quietly, "Did you hear that?"

312

Media Literacy

Recognize and Explain Purposes of Media

Media gives you information. It can also entertain you. There are many sources of media that are entertaining.

Practice It! Tell the class about something you saw, heard, or read in the media. Name the media. Were you entertained by it? Did it tell you information?

Tips

Listening ...

• Ask relevant questions to clarify what you hear.

Speaking ...

• Explain how words affect meaning in media.

Teamwork ...

• Follow rules for discussion.

Common Core State Standards

Language 6. Use words and phrases acquired through conversations, reading and being read to, and responding to texts, including using adjectives and adverbs to describe (e.g., *When other kids are happy that makes me happy*).
Also Speaking/Listening 1.

Oral Vocabulary

Let's Talk About

Solving Problems

- Share information about solving problems.

- Share ideas about helping those in need.

READING STREET ONLINE
CONCEPT TALK VIDEO
www.ReadingStreet.com

You've learned
0 7 2
Amazing Words
so far this year!

315

Common Core State Standards
Spiral Review Foundational Skills 2.
Demonstrate understanding of spoken words, syllables, and sounds (phonemes).

Phonemic Awareness

Let's Listen for

Sounds

- Find five things that contain the long *a* sound.

- Find the picture of the pail. Change the sound /l/ in *pail* to the sound /n/. Say the new word.

- Find the picture of the train. Say the sound at the end of *train*.

- The boat has a sail. Find something else that ends with the same sound as *sail*.

READING STREET ONLINE
SOUND-SPELLING CARDS
www.ReadingStreet.com

317

Common Core State Standards
Foundational Skills 3.b. Know spelling-sound correspondences for additional common vowel teams.
Also Foundational Skills 3.c., 3.f.

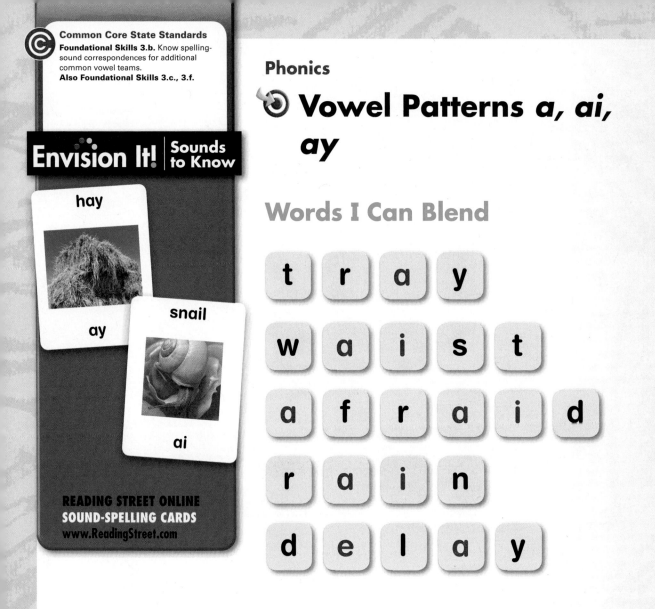

Envision It! | Sounds to Know

hay

ay

snail

ai

READING STREET ONLINE
SOUND-SPELLING CARDS
www.ReadingStreet.com

Phonics

Vowel Patterns *a, ai, ay*

Words I Can Blend

t r a y

w a i s t

a f r a i d

r a i n

d e l a y

Sentences I Can Read

1. Mark sets his lunch on a tray.

2. That belt fits around her waist.

3. Is Jill afraid this rain will delay her game?

318

I Can Read!

On Sunday, Craig heard a tap at his door. "Sorry, I'll just take a minute," Craig stated. Craig heard his pal Jay say behind the door, "Promise that you'll stay still everybody!" Craig got afraid to open that door. What kind of game was Jay playing? He waited a bit more. Then Craig went and opened the door. "Happy Birthday, Craig!" that big gang wailed. That bunch trailed in. They brought a party and stayed the rest of that day.

You've learned

◎ Vowel Patterns *a*, *ai*, *ay*

High-Frequency Words
behind   brought   door
everybody   minute   promise
sorry

One Good Turn Deserves Another Mexico

told by Judy Sierra
illustrated by Will Terry

Folk tale is a story that has been handed down over many years. Now you will read about how a coyote helps a mouse.

Question of the Week

How can we work together to solve problems?

Hop, stop, sniff. Hop, stop, sniff. A mouse was going across the desert. Suddenly, she heard a voice, "Help! Help me!" The sound came from under a rock. "Pleasssse get me out of here," said the voice with an unmistakable hiss.

The mouse placed her front paws against the rock. She was small, but she brought her best to the job. The rock rolled aside like a door opening. Out slid a snake.

"Thank you sssso much," said the snake as he
coiled around the mouse. "I was stuck under that
rock for a long time. I am very hungry."

"But you wouldn't eat me," squeaked the mouse.

"Why not?" the snake asked.

"Because I moved the rock," said the mouse. "I saved your life."

"So?" hissed the snake.

"So, one good turn deserves another," the mouse said hopefully.

The snake moved his head from side to side. "You are young," he said. "You don't know much about the world. Good is often repaid with evil."

"That's not fair!" cried the mouse.

"Everybody knows I am right," said the snake. "If you find even one creature who agrees with you, I promise to set you free."

325

A crow flew up behind them. "Uncle," said the snake to the crow, "help us settle an argument. I was trapped under a rock, and this silly mouse set me free. Now she thinks I shouldn't eat her."

"He should be grateful," the mouse insisted.

"Well, now," said the crow. "I've flown high and I've flown low. I've been just about everywhere. This morning, I ate some grasshoppers that were destroying a farmer's crops. Was he grateful? No, he used me for target practice! Good is often repaid with evil." And off he flew.

An armadillo ambled by. "What's all the noise?" she asked.

"Merely a minute of conversation before dinner," replied the snake. "My young friend moved a rock and set me free. Now she thinks I shouldn't eat her."

"One good turn deserves another," said the mouse.

"Wait a minute," said the armadillo. "Did you know he was a snake before you moved that rock?

"I guess I did, but…"

"Sorry, a snake is always a snake," the armadillo declared as she waddled away.

"That settles it," said the snake. "Everybody agrees with me."

"Can't we ask just one more creature?"
the mouse pleaded.

"I don't think you'll ever understand,"
groaned the snake.

A coyote trotted up. "Understand what?" he asked.

"The snake was trapped under that rock," the mouse explained.

"Which rock?" asked the coyote.

"Over there. That rock," said the snake.

"Oh," said the coyote. "The mouse was under that rock."

"No, I was under that rock!" said the snake.

"A snake under a rock? Impossible," the coyote snorted. "I have never seen such a thing."

The snake slid into the hole where he had been trapped. "I was in this hole," he hissed, "and that rock was on top of me!"

"This rock?" the coyote asked as he lifted his paw and pushed the rock on top of the snake.

"Yess!" hissed the snake. "Now show him, little mouse! Show him how you set me free."

But the mouse was already far away. "Thank you, cousin," she called as she ran. "I'll return the favor someday."

"Yes, indeed," said the coyote. "One good turn deserves another."

Common Core State Standards
Literature 2. Recount stories, including fables and folktales from diverse cultures, and determine their central message, lesson, or moral. **Also Literature 1.**

Envision It! Retell

Think Critically

1. What are other stories you have read where the animals act like people? Text to Text

2. What message do you think the author is trying to give you in this story? Author's Purpose

3. What characters think alike? What characters think differently? Compare and Contrast

4. Why does the coyote want to get the snake to slither back under the rock? Inferring

5. Look Back and Write
Look back at pages 324–325. What does the mouse mean by "one good turn deserves another"? Provide evidence to support your answer.

Key Ideas and Details • Text Evidence

About the Author and the Illustrator

Judy Sierra

As a child, Judy Sierra loved telling stories and putting on shows. She still does. Her books draw on this experience. She says, "Writing is a job, and there are many difficult and frustrating times. The most enjoyable part of being a writer is spending time with children and adults who love to read."

Will Terry

Will Terry studied illustration in college, and his pictures have appeared in books, magazines, and advertising. Mr. Terry and his family love snowboarding, mountain biking, and camping.

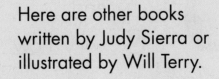

Here are other books written by Judy Sierra or illustrated by Will Terry.

Use the Reading Log in the *Reader's and Writer's Notebook* to record your independent reading.

Common Core State Standards
Writing 3. Write narratives in which they recount a well-elaborated event or short sequence of events, include details to describe actions, thoughts, and feelings, use temporal words to signal event order, and provide a sense of closure. **Also Language 2.c.**

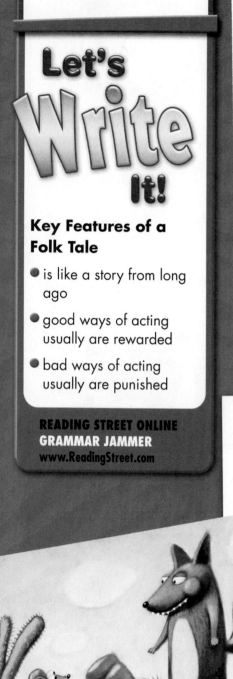

Let's Write It!

Key Features of a Folk Tale

- is like a story from long ago
- good ways of acting usually are rewarded
- bad ways of acting usually are punished

READING STREET ONLINE
GRAMMAR JAMMER
www.ReadingStreet.com

Folk Tale

A **folk tale** is a story like the stories told long ago. The student model on the next page is an example of a folk tale.

Writing Prompt Think about problems that happen when we don't work together. Now write a folk tale about animals that won't work together.

Writer's Checklist

Remember, you should . . .

☑ write a folk tale with a beginning, middle, and end.

☑ vary how you start the sentences.

☑ spell possessive nouns, using apostrophes.

338

Acorns for Dinner

Rat spent the day at Squirrel's house. For dinner, Squirrel put acorns in a pot. Rat took the acorns out.

"I do not like acorns," Rat said.

"I love acorns," said Squirrel.

"I will not eat acorns!" yelled Rat.

"I will only eat acorns!" yelled Squirrel.

The animals' fight did not stop. So they both had no dinner.

Single **possessive nouns** end in an apostrophe and **s**.

Writing Trait Sentences
The sentences begin in different ways.

Genre
In **folk tales**, bad actions often are punished.

Conventions

 ## Possessive Nouns

Remember A **possessive noun** shows who or what owns something.

 a **dog's** tail   two **dogs'** tails

339

Common Core State Standards
Literature 2. Recount stories, including fables and folktales from diverse cultures, and determine their central message, lesson, or moral. Also Literature 5.

Genre
Folk Tale/Fable

- A fable is a kind of folk tale. It is a very short story that teaches a lesson.

- A fable usually states its lesson, or theme, at the end of the story.

- The characters in fables are often animals.

- Read "The Lion and the Mouse." Look for elements that make this story a fable.

The Lion and the Mouse

retold by Claire Daniel
illustrated by Dan Andreasen

One day Mouse bumped into Lion by mistake and woke him up. Lion caught Mouse and dangled him by his tail.

"Do not eat me!" Mouse cried. "One day I will return the favor."

Lion laughed so hard that he dropped Mouse. Lion said, "How can a tiny mouse ever help a mighty lion like me?"

340

The next day Lion fell into a hunter's trap. He was covered with a net. Lion's roars shook the ground.

Other animals heard Lion, but no one wanted to come near an angry lion. Only Mouse ran toward Lion.

Mouse said, "I will help you."

Lion roared, "You are too small to help me!"

Let's Think About...

Why do you think Mouse goes near the "angry lion"?
Folk Tale/Fable

341

Let's Think About...

Compare these characters with the characters from the folk tale *One Good Turn Deserves Another.*
Folk Tale/Fable

Let's Think About...

Was Lion wrong about Mouse? How does Mouse help Lion?
Folk Tale/Fable

Mouse just said, "Lion, be quiet." Mouse chewed the net. He chewed for a long time. Finally, Mouse made a hole. Lion was free!

Just then the hunters returned. Lion roared at the men, and they ran away.

One hunter looked back. He saw the proud lion walking away. The hunter rubbed his eyes. Could it be? A mouse was riding on the lion's back!

Lion and Mouse became best friends. Lion liked to say, "Little friends can make the best friends."

Let's **Think** About...

Compare the setting and plot with those of the folk tale *One Good Turn Deserves Another.*
Folk Tale/Fable

Let's **Think** About...

Reading Across Texts The theme of the fable is the lesson it teaches. What are the themes of "The Lion and the Mouse" and *One Good Turn Deserves Another?*

Writing Across Texts Also think about the characters and settings. Write a paragraph comparing and contrasting the tales.

Common Core State Standards
Language 4.a. Use sentence-level context as a clue to the meaning of a word or phrase.
Also Foundational Skills 4.b., Speaking/Listening 3.

Vocabulary

While reading, you may read **unfamiliar words**. Look at the nearby words and pictures to find the relevant meaning.

Practice It! Read each group of sentences. Use other words to find the relevant meaning of each bold word.

1. The water in the **kettle** was hot. The cook made soup in the pot.

2. The puppy had a **sore** paw. It hurt him to walk on the paw.

Fluency

Read with Accuracy

Read every word you see. Do not skip any of them. Try to make no mistakes. Then, you will understand what you are reading.

Practice It! Read these sentences aloud.

1. Foxes, lizards, and snakes live in the desert.

2. A desert is a very dry place.

344

Listening and Speaking

Read all these instructions to a friend. Then have your friend follow them.

Give and Follow Instructions

To give instructions, tell each step in order. Tell what you do first, next, and last. When listening, ask questions to be sure you understand each step.

Practice It! First stand up. Then put your hands in the air and wave them. Now put your hands down. Next turn left and face the back of the room. Finally, turn right to face the front of the room.

Tips

Speaking . . .

• Speak clearly when giving oral instructions.

Teamwork . . .

• If you do not remember which step comes next, ask for the speaker to repeat the directions.

• Restate instructions.

345

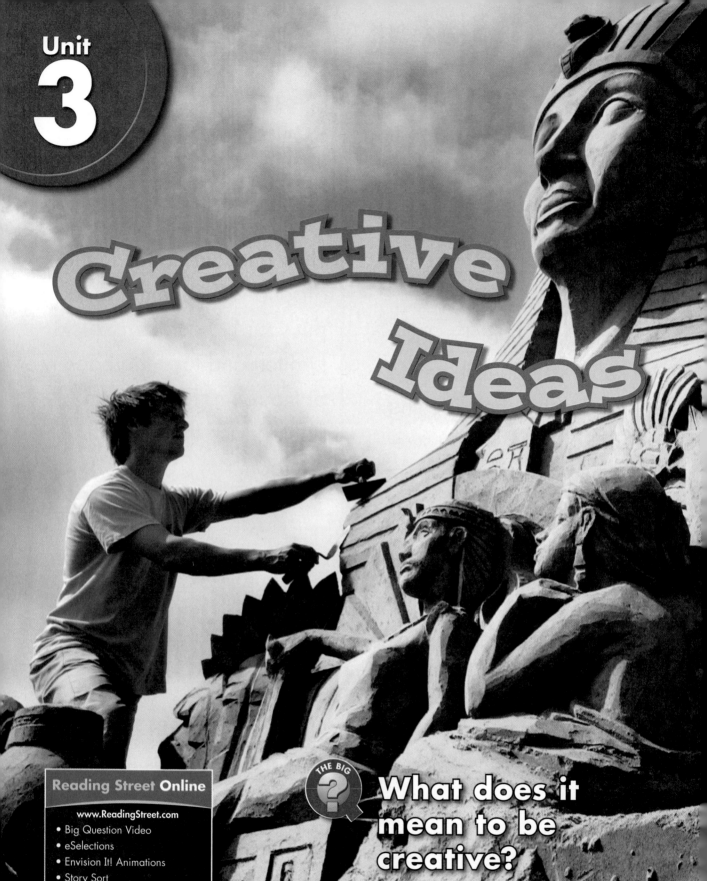

Unit
3

Creative
Ideas

What does it mean to be creative?

Oral Vocabulary

Let's Talk About

Creative Ideas

- Share information about helping creative ideas turn into inventions.

- Share ideas about helping projects get completed.

READING STREET ONLINE
CONCEPT TALK VIDEO
www.ReadingStreet.com

349

Common Core State Standards
Spiral Review Foundational Skills 2.
Demonstrate understanding of spoken
words, syllables, and sounds (phonemes).

Phonemic Awareness

Let's Listen for

Sounds

- Find five things that contain the long *e* sound.

- Find a team that is building a racer. Change the sound /m/ in *team* to the sound /ch/. Say the new word.

- Find something that rhymes with *meet*. Say the word. Now say each sound in the word.

READING STREET ONLINE
SOUND-SPELLING CARDS
www.ReadingStreet.com

350

351

Common Core State Standards

Foundational Skills 3.b. Know spelling-sound correspondences for additional common vowel teams. **Also Foundational Skills 3.a., 3.c., 3.f.**

Envision It! | Sounds to Know

easel

ea

bee

bunny

ee

-y

we

-e

**READING STREET ONLINE
SOUND-SPELLING CARDS**
www.ReadingStreet.com

Phonics

Vowel Patterns *e, ee, ea, y*

Words I Can Blend

w e

s w e e p

c l e a n

f u n n y

e a s y

Sentences I Can Read

1. We will sweep and clean those steps this morning.

2. Please tell us a funny joke.

3. This bread is easy to make.

I Can Read!

"Please watch your feet!" that man stated.
Steve peeked at his shoe and noted that it
had gotten wet. I guess he needed to step
over a small stream.

Last week Steve's science team won a trip. It
was neat! On that sunny day his teacher took
them to a pretty village not far from home.
That village had springs where water leaves
the ground. That water reaches rivers. Big
wheels use that water to make energy. Now
Steve and his team can teach others what
he learned.

You've learned

⊙ Vowel Patterns e, *ee, ea, y*

High-Frequency Words
guess   pretty   science   shoe
village   watch   won

Pearl and Wagner

Two Good Friends

by Kate McMullan · illustrated by R. W. Alley

Genre **Fantasy** is a make-believe story that could never happen in the real world.

Plants love music.
See the effect of
music on plan
the pot m

Question of the Week

When does support from others help with a creative idea?

355

The Robot

Everyone in Ms. Star's class was talking about the Science Fair.

"I am going to make a robot," said Pearl.

"I am going to win a prize," said Wagner.

Pearl got to work. She taped up the flaps
of a great big box. She cut a hole in the top.
Then she cut a hole in the lid of a shoe box.
She glued the shoe box lid to the top of the
great big box. Wagner held the boxes together
while the glue dried.

"Maybe I will make a walkie-talkie," he said.

Pearl punched a hole in one end of the shoe box. She stuck string through the hole. She tied the string in a knot.

"Maybe I will make a brain out of clay," said Wagner.

"Cool," said Pearl.

She drew eyes and a nose on the shoe box. Wagner looked at the shoe box.

"The eyes are too small," he said.

Pearl made the eyes bigger.

"Maybe I will make a rocket," said Wagner. "*Vrooom!* Blast off!"

Pearl put the shoe box onto the lid.

"There!" she said. "Finished!"
Pearl pulled the string.
The robot's mouth opened.
She threw in a wad of paper.
Then she let go of the string.
The robot's mouth shut.
   "Wow!" said Wagner.
"A trash-eating robot!"

"Let's see what everyone has made," said Ms. Star.

"Uh-oh," said Wagner. He had not made anything yet.

Lulu raised her hand. "I made a walkie-talkie," she said.

"I was going to do that!" said Wagner.

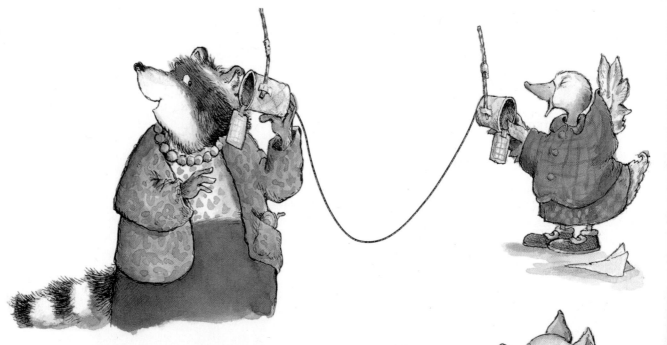

"I made paper airplanes," said Bud. "This chart shows how far they flew."

Wagner slapped his head. "Why didn't *I* think of that?"

Henry showed how to get electricity from a potato.

"Henry is a brain," said Pearl.

"Pearl?" Wagner said. "Remember how I held the boxes together while the glue dried?"

"I remember," said Pearl.

"Remember how I told you to give the robot bigger eyes?" asked Wagner.

Pearl nodded. "I remember."

"Your turn, Pearl," said Ms. Star.

"I made a trash-eating robot," said Pearl. She looked at Wagner. He was slumped down in his seat.

"Wagner and I made it together," said Pearl.

Wagner sat right up again.

Pearl pulled the robot's string. She pulled too hard. The robot's head fell off.

"Uh-oh," said Wagner.

"I guess you two friends have more work to do," said Ms. Star.

"I guess so," said Pearl. "But I don't mind, because Wagner and I will do all of the work together."

"Uh-oh," said Wagner.

The Science Fair

On Science Fair Day, Pearl and Wagner were still working on their robot. Pearl stretched rubber bands. She held them tight. Wagner stapled them onto the shoe box and the lid.

"That should do it," he said.

Pearl and Wagner hurried to the gym with their robot. They passed a boy with an ant village. They passed a girl playing music for plants. They passed Henry. He had his electric potato hooked up to a tiny Ferris wheel.

Pearl and Wagner set
up their robot.

A judge came over.

"Watch this," said
Pearl. Pearl pulled
the robot's string. Nothing happened.
She pulled harder. The robot's mouth popped
open. The rubber bands flew everywhere.

"Yikes!" said the judge.

"Oh, no!" said Wagner. "There goes our prize!"

"We are not quite ready," Pearl told the judge.

"I will come back in five minutes,"
said the judge.

"I have more rubber bands in my desk," said Pearl. She raced off to get them.

Wagner tapped his foot. He bit his nails. Pearl was taking forever! The judge would be back any second. He had to *do* something.

Wagner looked around. No one was watching him. He pulled the tape off the big box. He opened the back of the robot and slipped inside.

The judge came back. She did not see
Pearl and Wagner. She started to leave.

"Wait!" said the robot.

"Oh, my stars!" said the judge.

"A talking robot!"

Just then Pearl came back.

"You have a nice smile," the robot was telling the judge. "And such pretty eyes."

"Do you think so?" said the judge.

Pearl could not believe her ears.

"Your robot is so smart!" said the judge. "How does it work?"

"Uh . . ." said Pearl. "It is hard to explain."

The judge opened the robot's mouth. She looked inside.

"Hi there!" said Wagner.

"Uh-oh," said Pearl.

The judge gave out the prizes. The girl who
played music for plants won first prize. Henry
and his electric potato won second prize. The
trash-eating robot did not win any prize at all.

"I was only trying to help," Wagner told Pearl.
"I know," said Pearl. "You are a good friend,
Wagner. And you were a pretty good robot too."

Common Core State Standards

Literature 1. Ask and answer such questions as *who, what, where, when, why,* and *how* to demonstrate understanding of key details in a text. **Also Literature 2., Writing 8.**

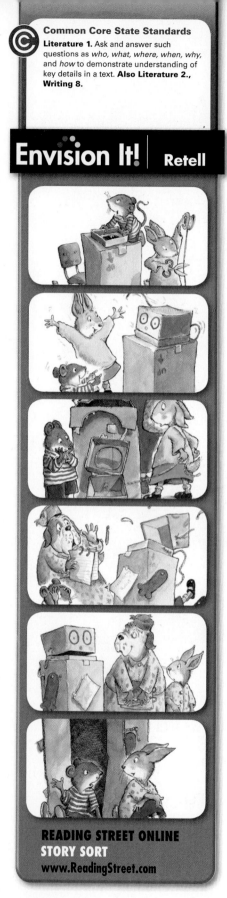

Envision It! | Retell

**READING STREET ONLINE
STORY SORT**
www.ReadingStreet.com

Think Critically

1. Pearl and Wagner helped each other. How do you help your friends? Text to Self

2. Was the author trying to make you laugh, explain something, or give you information? Explain. Author's Purpose

3. What message is the author trying to give you about friends? Author's Purpose

4. What questions did you ask yourself as you read? How did you find the answers to your questions? Questioning

5. Look Back and Write
Look back at page 369. Why do you think the talking robot didn't win a prize? Provide evidence to support your answer.

Key Ideas and Details • Text Evidence

Meet the Author and the Illustrator

Kate McMullan

Kate McMullan loves to read. When asked what she wanted to be when she grew up, she always said, "A reader." When she decided to try writing, she moved to New York City.

R. W. Alley

R. W. Alley has illustrated many books for children. He says Kate McMullan had been thinking of a dog and a cat as Pearl and Wagner. But when she saw his mouse and his rabbit, she approved.

Here are other books by Kate McMullan.

Use the Reading Log in the *Reader's and Writer's Notebook* to record your independent reading.

Common Core State Standards

Writing 3. Write narratives in which they recount a well-elaborated event or short sequence of events, include details to describe actions, thoughts, and feelings, use temporal words to signal event order, and provide a sense of closure. **Also Language 1.**

Let's Write It!

Key Features of an Animal Fantasy

- characters are animals
- events are make-believe
- characters do things that real animals cannot do

READING STREET ONLINE
GRAMMAR JAMMER
www.ReadingStreet.com

Narrative

Animal Fantasy

An **animal fantasy** is a story with events that cannot really happen. The student model on the next page is an example of an animal fantasy.

Writing Prompt Think about how people help with creative ideas. Now write a story about animal characters who create something together.

Writer's Checklist

Remember, you should . . .

✓ tell about animals who act like people.

✓ express your ideas and your style of writing.

✓ use verbs correctly.

The Flying Machine

Dog and Cat watch the birds in the sky. They wish they could fly too.

"Let's build a flying machine," says Dog.

First, they make a place to sit. Then they add wings. Next, Dog and Cat wait for the wind. The wind carries them up into the air.

"We're flying!" says Cat.

Verbs show action.

Genre This **animal fantasy** tells about actions real animals cannot do.

Writing Trait Voice The writer shows an interest in flying.

Conventions

 ### Verbs

Remember A word that shows action is a **verb**. The word **make** is a verb.

Pearl and Wagner **make** a robot.

375

Science in Reading

Genre
Autobiography

- An autobiography is the true story of a person's life written by that person.

- An autobiography is an example of literary nonfiction.

- An autobiography uses words such as *I* and *me*.

Alberto,
the Scientist

My name is Alberto. I like science. It has always been my favorite subject. Even when I was a baby, I tested things. I would give my food to our dog. If Millie ate it, I would too.

When I got older, I tested to see which soap cleaned dishes better. I checked to see which light bulb lasted longer. I even tested pencils to see which was the hardest to break. Mom and Dad liked the tests. They said every family could use a scientist.

Every year, we have a science project to do in school. This is a fun time. We think of an experiment. We guess how it will turn out. Then we test it.

In first grade, I liked to grow things. I planted seeds. I wanted to see how they would grow. I put some seeds in the light. I kept others in the dark. I kept some seeds very dry. I kept others wet. It was fun to see which seeds grew the best.

Let's Think About...

How can you tell that this story is an autobiography?
Autobiography

377

Let's **Think** About...

What do you think is the main idea that Alberto wants you to know?
Autobiography

Let's **Think** About...

How did Alberto's interests change as he got older?
Autobiography

In second grade, I loved space. I liked to go outside at night. I liked to look up at all the stars and planets. I wanted to ride in spaceships. I wanted to go to the moon. I had a book about the moon. I learned about an eclipse.

An eclipse is when Earth's shadow crosses the moon. You can't see the moon then. I showed the class how it happens. Randy helped me. We used a flashlight, a big ball, and a globe. Our teacher said we did a very good job. We made a good team.

What will my next project be?
I think I'll do a weather study. I will
write down the temperature and
rainfall where I live. I will see how
it changes over time. My mom said
she will help me use a thermometer.
Dad is going to show me how to
find out exactly how much rain falls.
They both say I'd be a great weather
reporter. I can't wait to begin.

Let's **Think** About...

How can you
distinguish this
nonfiction piece
from fiction?
Autobiography

Let's **Think** About...

**Reading Across
Texts** Were the
science projects in
*Pearl and Wagner:
Two Good Friends*
and "Alberto, the
Scientist"
successful?
Compare them.

**Writing Across
Texts** What
would you do for
a science project?
Write a paragraph
telling what you
would do and why.

Common Core State Standards
Foundational Skills 4.b. Read on-level text orally with accuracy, appropriate rate, and expression on successive readings. **Also Speaking/Listening 6., Language 5.**

Let's Learn It!

READING STREET ONLINE
VOCABULARY ACTIVITIES
www.ReadingStreet.com

Vocabulary

An **antonym** is a word that means the opposite of another word.

wet

dry

Wet and *dry* are antonyms.

Practice It! Read these words. Think of an antonym for each word. Write sentences using the antonyms.

new   hot   easy   dirty

Fluency

Read with Appropriate Rate

Read as though you are speaking. Do not read too fast or too slow.

Practice It! Read these sentences aloud.

1. Blue jays are very big birds that make lots of noise.

2. My friends are Jerome, Kim, Nico, and Sasha.

Listening and Speaking

Speak clearly when making introductions.

Make Introductions

When making introductions, you should name each person and tell something about each person. Use verbs such as *meet* and *introduce*. Speak clearly and at the right pace. You want the people to understand each other's name.

Practice It! Introduce two classmates to each other. Be sure to tell their names and something about them. Use verbs. Take turns making and listening to introductions.

Tips

Listening . . .

- Listen carefully for the person's name when you are being introduced to someone.

Speaking . . .

- Use proper conventions when speaking.

Common Core State Standards

Language 6. Use words and phrases acquired through conversations, reading and being read to, and responding to texts, including using adjectives and adverbs to describe (e.g., *When other kids are happy that makes me happy*).
Also Speaking/Listening 1.

Oral Vocabulary

Let's Talk About

Creative Ways to Communicate

- Share information about signs and symbols to communicate.

- Share ideas about speaking and writing to communicate.

READING STREET ONLINE
CONCEPT TALK VIDEO
www.ReadingStreet.com

Common Core State Standards
Spiral Review Foundational Skills 2.
Demonstrate understanding of spoken
words, syllables, and sounds (phonemes).

Phonemic Awareness

Let's Listen for

Sounds

- Find five things that contain the long *o* sound.

- Find the boy's coat. Change the long *o* sound in *coat* to a short *a* sound. Say the new word and find it in the picture.

- Find something that rhymes with *load*. Say the word. Now say the last sound in the word.

384

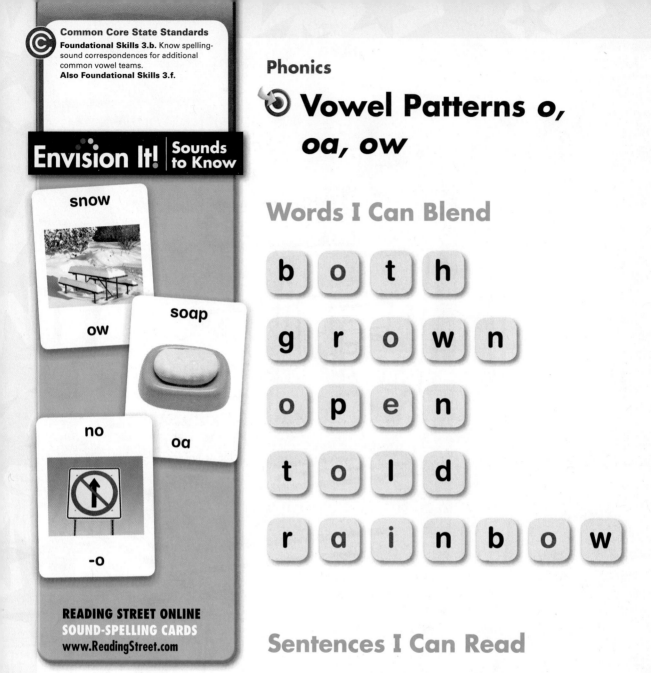

Envision It! Sounds to Know

snow

ow

soap

oa

no

-o

Phonics

🎯 Vowel Patterns o, oa, ow

Words I Can Blend

b o t h

g r o w n

o p e n

t o l d

r a i n b o w

Sentences I Can Read

1. These girls have both grown since last year.

2. Will Cole open his store?

3. Mom told us, "Look at that rainbow!"

I Can Read!

At school, Joan's teacher asked her class to sketch a picture. "Which faraway places would you most like to go?" No answer came to Joan's mind. She showed her parents that paper later. "Would you visit the coast and take a boat trip, or go places with cold and snow?" her mom asked, as Joan helped her wash dishes. Joan didn't have a goal of going to faraway places, she told her mom. She just wants to be in close company with people she's grown to like.

You've learned

⊙ Vowel Patterns o, oa, ow

High-Frequency Words
answer   company   faraway
parents   picture   school   wash

Dear Juno

by Soyung Pak

illustrated by Susan Kathleen Hartung

 **Genre**

Realistic fiction tells about made-up events that could happen in real life. This next story is about Juno, a boy who finds a creative way to write to his grandmother.

Question of the Week

In what creative ways do we communicate?

Juno watched as the red and white blinking lights soared across the night sky like shooting stars, and waited as they disappeared into faraway places. Juno wondered where they came from. He wondered where they were going. And he wondered if any of the planes came from a little town near Seoul where his grandmother lived, and where she ate persimmons every evening before bed.

Juno looked at the letter that came that day. It was long and white and smudged. He saw the red and blue marks on the edges and knew the letter came from far away. His name and address were neatly printed on the front, so he knew the letter was for him. But best of all, the special stamp on the corner told Juno that the letter was from his grandmother.

Through the window Juno could see his parents. He saw bubbles growing in the sink. He saw dirty dishes waiting to be washed. He knew he would have to wait for the cleaning to be done before his parents could read the letter to him.

"Maybe I can read the inside too," Juno said
to his dog, Sam. Sam wagged his tail. Very
carefully, Juno opened the envelope. Inside, he
found a letter folded into a neat, small square.

He unfolded it. Tucked inside were a picture
and a dried flower.

Juno looked at the letters and words he couldn't understand. He pulled out the photograph. It was a picture of his grandmother holding a cat. He pulled out the red and yellow flower. It felt light and gentle like a dried leaf. Juno smiled. "C'mon, Sam," Juno said. "Let's find Mom and Dad."

395

"Grandma has a new cat," Juno said as he handed the letter to his mother. "And she's growing red and yellow flowers in her garden."

"How do you know she has a new cat?" Juno's father asked.

"She wouldn't send me a picture of a strange cat," said Juno.

"I guess not," said Juno's father.

"How do you know the flower is from her garden?" asked Juno's mother.

"She wouldn't send me a flower from someone else's garden," Juno answered.

"No, she wouldn't," said Juno's mother.

Then Juno's mother read him the letter.

396

Dear Juno,

How are you? I have a new cat to keep me company. *I named him Juno after you. He can't help me weed, but the rabbits no longer come to eat my flowers.*

Grandma

"Just like you read it yourself," Juno's father said.

"I did read it," Juno said.

"Yes, you did," said his mother.

At school, Juno showed his class his grandmother's picture and dried flower. His teacher even pinned the letter to the board. All day long, Juno kept peeking at the flower from his grandmother's garden. He didn't have a garden that grew flowers, but he had a swinging tree.

Juno looked at the letter pinned to the board. Did his grandmother like getting letters too? Yes, Juno thought. She likes getting letters just like I do. So Juno decided to write one.

After school, Juno ran to his backyard. He picked a leaf from the swinging tree—the biggest leaf he could find.

Juno found his mother, who was sitting at her desk. He showed her the leaf. "I'm going to write a letter," he told her.

"I'm sure it will be a very nice letter," she answered, and gave him a big yellow envelope.

"Yes it will," Juno said, and then he began to draw.

First, he drew a picture of his mom and dad
standing outside the house. Second, he drew
a picture of Sam playing underneath his big
swinging tree. Then very carefully, Juno drew a
picture of himself standing under an airplane in
a starry, nighttime sky. After he was finished, he
placed everything in the envelope.

"Here's my letter," Juno announced proudly.
"You can read it if you want."

Juno's father looked in the envelope.

He pulled out the leaf. "Only a big swinging tree could grow a leaf this big," he said.

Juno's mother pulled out one of the drawings. "What a fine picture," she said. "It takes a good artist to say so much with a drawing."

Juno's father patted Juno on the head. "It's just like a real letter," he said.

"It is a real letter," Juno said.

"It certainly is," said his mother. Then they mailed the envelope and waited.

One day a big envelope came. It was from Juno's grandmother. This time, Juno didn't wait at all. He opened the envelope right away.

Inside, Juno found a box of colored pencils. He knew she wanted another letter.

Next, he pulled out a picture of his grandmother. He noticed she was sitting with a cat and two kittens. He thought for a moment and laughed. Now his grandmother would have to find a new name for her cat—in Korea, Juno was a boy's name, not a girl's.

Then he pulled out a small toy plane.

Juno smiled. His grandmother was coming to visit.

"Maybe she'll bring her cat when she comes to visit," Juno said to Sam as he climbed into bed. "Maybe you two will be friends."

404

Soon Juno was fast asleep. And when he dreamed that night, he dreamed about a faraway place, a village just outside Seoul, where his grandmother, whose gray hair sat on top of her head like a powdered doughnut, was sipping her morning tea.

The cool air feels crisp against her cheek. Crisp enough to crackle, he dreams, like the golden leaves which cover the persimmon garden.

Envision It! Retell

**READING STREET ONLINE
STORY SORT**
www.ReadingStreet.com

Think Critically

1. Juno sends a letter to his grandmother. Whom would you send a letter to? What would you say in the letter?

Text to Self

2. Why do you think the author tells about letters without words? Author's Purpose

3. How does Juno feel about his grandmother? Explain why you think he feels this way.

Draw Conclusions/Make Inferences

4. What picture did you have in your mind each time Juno spoke of his grandmother? Visualize

5. Look Back and Write
Look back at page 391. How does Juno know who sent the letter? Provide evidence to support your answer.

Key Ideas and Details • Text Evidence

Meet the Author and the Illustrator

Soyung Pak

Soyung Pak was born in South Korea. When she was two years old, she moved to New Jersey. When a plane flew overhead, her family waved. They pretended Grandmother was on the plane, coming from Korea.

Susan Kathleen Hartung

Susan Hartung has always loved to draw. As a child, she sometimes got in trouble for her pictures. Finally she learned to do her drawings on paper!

Here are other books by Soyung Pak.

Use the Reading Log in the *Reader's and Writer's Notebook* to record your independent reading.

Common Core State Standards
Writing 3. Write narratives in which they recount a well-elaborated event or short sequence of events, include details to describe actions, thoughts, and feelings, use temporal words to signal event order, and provide a sense of closure.
Also Language 1., 2.b.

Let's Write It!

Key Features of a Friendly Letter

- includes the date, a greeting, the body, a closing, and a signature
- the body of the letter has the message
- tells the writer's ideas and feelings

READING STREET ONLINE
GRAMMAR JAMMER
www.ReadingStreet.com

Expository

Friendly Letter

A **friendly letter** expresses a message to someone the writer knows. The student model on the next page is an example of a friendly letter.

Writing Prompt Think about the different ways people communicate. Now write a friendly letter to a friend or classmate about a new way to communicate.

Writer's Checklist

Remember, you should . . .

☑ write a letter with a date, greeting, and closing.

☑ have each sentence focus on the main idea.

☑ spell verbs correctly.

January 10, 2011

Dear Sam,

Gram sent my brothers a text message. She used her new phone. She wants them to come to my soccer game. Gram told them when the game starts. I hope they get the message and see me play.

Your friend,

Anna

Conventions

Verbs with Nouns

Remember Add **-s** to verbs with singular subjects. Do not add **-s** if the subject is plural.

Anna **writes**. Authors **write**.

409

Common Core State Standards
Literature 1. Ask and answer such
questions as *who, what, where, when, why,*
and *how* to demonstrate understanding of
key details in a text.

Genre
Historical Fiction

- Historical fiction is a realistic story that takes place in the past.

- Historical fiction uses events that could have really happened.

- Historical fiction mixes real facts from the past with a made-up story.

- Read "Many Ways to Be a Soldier." Look for historical facts and elements of fiction in the story.

Many Ways to Be a Soldier

written by Wendy Pfeffer
illustrated by Paul Weiner

September 19, 1776   Stites Point, New Jersey

For many days, Rem had seen the men meeting in town. He had heard them whispering words like "redcoats" and "war." Redcoats were British soldiers. The American colonies were at war with Great Britain.

Let's **Think** About...

In what part of American history does the story take place? **Historical Fiction**

The Americans wanted freedom from Britain. So they rebelled against the British. British soldiers had come to America to fight back. British soldiers were everywhere. British warships patrolled the coast.

Rem slipped into his clothes. He raced down the ladder to the fireplace. A horn hung over the mantel. Rem grabbed the horn. Papa's sword was already gone. A few years ago, Grandfather proudly gave the sword to Rem's papa. He gave the horn to Rem for his birthday.

411

Grandfather told how his father had carried that horn in battle. He taught Rem how to blow songs and battle calls.

If Papa was going to battle, Rem was going too. Horn in hand, he ran out of the cabin. His dog, Toby, darted after him.

Let's Think About...

Why does Rem take the horn? How does he plan on using it? **Historical Fiction**

Rem heard noises near the trees. It sounded like footsteps. Could it be a Tory? Tories were loyal to Great Britain. They spied on the colonists. Then they reported to the redcoats.

It was only Rebecca, Rem's neighbor. "We have our cannon," said Rebecca, raising her spyglass. "And we know how to fire it." She put her spyglass down. Rem picked it up to look through it.

Rem saw a shadowy form on the water. It was moving closer and closer to Stites Point. Suddenly, Rem dropped the spyglass. "The redcoats are coming," he whispered.

"Sarah," Rebecca said. "Run up the flag. Let them think the troops are here."

Let's Think About...

Do you think these characters are real or fictional? Why? **Historical Fiction**

413

"Let me help!" cried Rem.

But Rebecca ignored him. She lit the cannon's fuse with the firebrand. As the fuse burned, Rem watched. He felt helpless. "They're getting close," said Rem. "They're almost at the beach!"

Let's **Think** About...

What are some real facts in this story? **Historical Fiction**

BOOOOOOOM!

The cannon fired. The little group on Foxborough Hill watched the cannonball zoom closer and closer to the enemy longboat. Then it passed over the redcoats' heads. Rebecca and Sarah began to reload the cannon. But they didn't have enough time. They needed help.

Rem did the only thing he could. He put the horn to his lips. He blasted out the call to arms. That call ordered soldiers to fight. The horn's wail rang out.

Suddenly, the longboat turned. "You fooled them," Rebecca said.

"They think our men are here, ready to fight," said Sarah.

Rem blew his horn until the longboat reached the British warship. He blew as the redcoats climbed aboard. The warship pulled up its anchor. It turned and sailed toward the ocean. The little group on Foxborough Hill cheered.

Rebecca patted Rem on the back. "Rem," she said, "You're a hero. Stites Point is safe."

Let's Think About...

What are some elements of fiction in the story?
Historical Fiction

Let's Think About...

Reading Across Texts In both *Dear Juno* and "Many Ways to Be a Soldier," characters wanted to send a message to others. What messages were they trying to send?

Writing Across Texts Write a paragraph telling what message each character sent and why.

415

Common Core State Standards
Language 4.b. Determine the meaning of the new word formed when a known prefix is added to a known word (e.g., *happy/unhappy, tell/retell*).
Also Foundational Skills 4., Speaking/Listening 1.a.

Let's **Learn** It!

**READING STREET ONLINE
VOCABULARY ACTIVITIES**
www.ReadingStreet.com

Vocabulary

A **prefix** is a word part added to the beginning of a word. A prefix changes the meaning of a word. The word part **dis-** is a prefix. The prefix **dis-** often means "not." The word **dislike** means "not like."

Practice It! Read and write each word. Underline the prefix. Then write the meaning of each word.

disallow   disobey   displease

Fluency

Accuracy and Appropriate Rate

When reading, do not add or leave out words as you read. If you read too fast, you may skip some words. Be sure you understand the reading.

Practice It! Read these sentences aloud.

My friends and I have fun in the winter. We like to build snow forts. We make snowmen to guard the fort.

416

Listening and Speaking

Listen carefully to ideas for solving problems.

Solve Problems

Sometimes you and your class may have a problem. What can you do? First, tell what the problem is. Make sure everyone understands the problem. Talk about ways to solve it. Listen to everyone's ideas. Choose the idea you think will work best. Together you can solve the problem.

Practice It! Imagine your class needs pictures or maps for a class book about the USA. Discuss the problem. Share ideas on how to solve it. Use verbs with singular and plural nouns. Listen to everyone's ideas. Then make a decision. What will the class do?

Tips

Listening ...

• Pay attention to the ideas of others as you discuss ways to solve problems.

Speaking ...

• Speak clearly when sharing your ideas.

Common Core State Standards

Language 6. Use words and phrases acquired through conversations, reading and being read to, and responding to texts, including using adjectives and adverbs to describe (e.g., *When other kids are happy that makes me happy*).
Also Speaking/Listening 1.

Oral Vocabulary

Let's Talk About

Creative Thinking

- Share information about using something in a different way.

- Share ideas about having a good plan.

**READING STREET ONLINE
CONCEPT TALK VIDEO**
www.ReadingStreet.com

418

Phonemic Awareness

Let's Listen for

Sounds

- Find five things that are compound words.

- Find the flagpole. Say each of the words that make up the compound word *flagpole*.

- Find another compound word and say the two words that make up that word. Now say each sound in those two words.

**READING STREET ONLINE
SOUND-SPELLING CARDS**
www.ReadingStreet.com

420

Common Core State Standards

Language 4.d. Use knowledge of the meaning of individual words to predict the meaning of compound words (e.g., *birdhouse, lighthouse, housefly; bookshelf, notebook, bookmark*). **Also Foundational Skills 3.f.**

Envision It! | Sounds to Know

football

compound word

**READING STREET ONLINE
SOUND-SPELLING CARDS**
www.ReadingStreet.com

Phonics

Compound Words

Words I Can Blend

b a c k y a r d

s a i l b o a t

d a y t i m e

s u n r i s e

p a s s w o r d

Sentences I Can Read

1. From Carl's backyard, he can see that sailboat on Sand Lake.

2. Daytime begins at sunrise.

3. Use this password to get in my fort.

Bonny had a very strange dream. In that dream, Dad saw her making pancakes in the driveway. Then Mom caught her eating popcorn in the backyard. Finally, Sis noticed her sending a postcard in her bedroom. It was a strange dream. It must have made Bonny very tired because today she woke up late. Whatever made her dream that? I believe it might have been the meatballs she ate before bed. Tomorrow she will not eat as many.

You've learned

⊙ Compound Words

High-Frequency Words
been believe caught finally
today tomorrow whatever

Anansi
Goes Fishing

retold by Eric A. Kimmel
illustrated by Janet Stevens

Genre

A **folk tale** is a story that has been handed down over many years. Now you will read about how Anansi the Spider is tricked by Turtle.

Question of the Week
How can creative thinking solve a problem?

One fine afternoon Anansi the Spider was
walking by the river when he saw his friend
Turtle coming toward him carrying a large fish.
Anansi loved to eat fish, though he was much too
lazy to catch them himself.

"Where did you get that fish?"
he asked Turtle.

"I caught it today when I went fishing,"
Turtle replied.

"I want to learn to catch fish too," Anansi
said. "Will you teach me?"

"Certainly!" said Turtle. "Meet me by the river
tomorrow. We will go fishing together. Two can
do twice the work of one."

But Anansi did not intend to do any work at all. "Turtle is slow and stupid," he said to himself. "I will trick him into doing all the work. Then I will take the fish for myself." But Turtle was not as stupid as Anansi thought.

Early the next morning, Turtle arrived. "Are you ready to get started, Anansi?" he asked.

"Yes!" Anansi said. "I have been waiting a long time. I want to learn to catch fish as well as you do."

427

"First we make a net," said Turtle. "Netmaking is hard work. When I do it myself, I work and get tired. But since there are two of us, we can share the task. One of us can work while the other gets tired."

"I don't want to get tired," Anansi said. "I'll make the net. You can get tired."

"All right," said Turtle. He showed Anansi how to weave a net. Then he lay down on the riverbank.

"This is hard work," Anansi said.

"I know," said Turtle, yawning. "I'm getting very tired."

Anansi worked all day weaving the net. The harder he worked, the more tired Turtle grew. Turtle yawned and stretched, and finally he went to sleep. After many hours the net was done.

"Wake up, Turtle," Anansi said. "The net is finished."

Turtle rubbed his eyes. "This net is strong and light. You are a fine netmaker, Anansi. I know you worked hard because I am very tired. I am so tired, I have to go home and sleep. Meet me here tomorrow. We will catch fish then."

The next morning Turtle met Anansi by the river again.

"Today we are going to set the net in the river," Turtle said. "That is hard work. Yesterday you worked while I got tired, so today I'll work while you get tired."

"No, no!" said Anansi. "I would rather work than get tired."

"All right," said Turtle. So while Anansi worked hard all day setting the net in the river, Turtle lay on the riverbank, getting so tired he finally fell asleep.

"Wake up, Turtle," Anansi said, hours later. "The net is set. I'm ready to start catching fish."

Turtle yawned. "I'm too tired to do any more today, Anansi. Meet me here tomorrow morning. We'll catch fish then."

Turtle met Anansi on the riverbank the next morning.

"I can hardly wait to catch fish," Anansi said.

"That's good," Turtle replied. "Catching fish is hard work. You worked hard these past two days, Anansi. I think I should work today and let you get tired."

"Oh, no!" said Anansi. "I want to catch fish. I don't want to get tired."

"All right," said Turtle. "Whatever you wish."

Anansi worked hard all day pulling the net out of the river while Turtle lay back, getting very, very tired.

432

How pleased Anansi was to find a large fish caught in the net!

"What do we do now?" he asked Turtle.

Turtle yawned. "Now we cook the fish. Cooking is hard work. I think I should cook while you get tired."

"No!" cried Anansi. He did not want to share any bit of the fish. "I will cook. You get tired."

   While Turtle watched, Anansi built a fire and
cooked the fish from head to tail.

   "That fish smells delicious," Turtle said. "You
are a good cook, Anansi. And you worked hard.
I know, because I am very, very tired. Now it is
time to eat the fish. When I eat by myself, I eat
and get full. Since there are two of us, we should
share the task. One of us should eat while the
other gets full. Which do you want to do?"

   "I want to get full!" Anansi said, thinking only
of his stomach.

   "Then I will eat." Turtle began to eat while
Anansi lay back and waited for his stomach to
get full.

"Are you full yet?" Turtle asked Anansi.
"Not yet. Keep eating."

Turtle ate some more. "Are you full yet?"
"No. Keep eating."

Turtle ate some more. "Are you full yet?"
"Not at all," Anansi said. "I'm as empty
as when you started."

"That's too bad," Turtle told him. "Because I'm full, and all the fish is gone."

"What?" Anansi cried. It was true. Turtle had eaten the whole fish. "You cheated me!" Anansi yelled when he realized what had happened.

"I did not!" Turtle replied.

"You did! You made me do all the work, then you ate the fish yourself. You won't get away with this. I am going to the Justice Tree."

Anansi ran to the Justice
Tree. Warthog sat beneath
its branches. Warthog was
a fair and honest judge. All
the animals brought their
quarrels to him.

"What do you want,
Anansi?" Warthog asked.

"I want justice," Anansi
said. "Turtle cheated me. We
went fishing together. He
tricked me into doing all the
work, then he ate the fish
himself. Turtle deserves to
be punished."

Warthog knew how lazy
Anansi was. He couldn't
imagine him working hard at
anything. "Did you really do
all the work?" he asked.

"Yes," Anansi replied.

"What did you do?"

439

"I wove the net.

I set it in the river.

I caught the fish,

and I cooked it."

"That is a lot of work. You must have gotten very tired."

"No," said Anansi. "I didn't get tired at all. Turtle got tired, not me."

Warthog frowned. "Turtle got tired? What did he do?"

"Nothing!"

"If he did nothing, why did he get tired? Anansi, I don't believe you. No one gets tired by doing nothing. If Turtle got tired, then he must have done all the work. You are not telling the truth. Go home now and stop making trouble."

Warthog had spoken. There was nothing more to be said. Anansi went home in disgrace, and it was a long time before he spoke to Turtle again.

But some good came out of it. Anansi learned how to weave nets and how to use them to catch food. He taught his friends how to do it, and they taught their friends. Soon spiders all over the world were weaving. To this day, wherever you find spiders, you will find their nets.

They are called "spider webs."

How to Tie
Knots

A stopper is a knot tied at the end of a rope. It is used to keep a rope from sliding through a hole.

The Overhand Knot is one type of stopper knot. It is a very simple knot to tie, but, once tightened, it is very hard to untie.

Try making this knot with a piece of string.

Overhand Knot

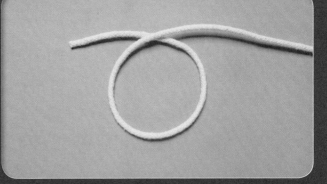

Make a loop with the string.

Pass one end of the string through the hole in the loop.

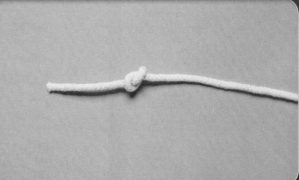

Tighten the knot by pulling on both ends at once.

Common Core State Standards
Literature 2. Recount stories, including fables and folktales from diverse cultures, and determine their central message, lesson, or moral.
Also Literature 1.

Envision It! Retell

**READING STREET ONLINE
STORY SORT**
www.ReadingStreet.com

Think Critically

1. How is the fishing net Anansi makes in the story like a spider's web? Text to World

2. Was the author trying to make you laugh, explain something, or give you information? Explain. Author's Purpose

3. Compare and contrast the story "A Fool Goes Fishing" on pages 306–311 with this story. How are they alike? How are they different?

Compare and Contrast

4. Retell each version in your own words. Summarize

5. Look Back and Write
Look back at page 435. Why does Anansi not feel full? Provide evidence to support your answer.

Key Ideas and Details • Text Evidence

Meet the Author and the Illustrator

Eric A. Kimmel

Eric A. Kimmel first heard stories about Anansi as a child in New York City. He also heard Anansi stories from neighbors when he lived in the Virgin Islands. The stories come from Africa and are very old. "I enjoyed telling the stories so much that I tried my hand at writing them."

Janet Stevens

Before Janet Stevens drew Anansi, she read books about spiders. She thought about how to show Anansi's personality. "I mainly did it through his movement and gestures. He doesn't have a lot of face." She didn't want Anansi to look cute.

Ms. Stevens has written and illustrated many children's books.

Here are other books by Eric A. Kimmel and by Janet Stevens.

Anansi and the Moss-Covered Rock
retold by Eric A. Kimmel
illustrated by Janet Stevens

The TOWN MOUSE & the COUNTRY MOUSE
AN AESOP FABLE
ADAPTED AND ILLUSTRATED BY
JANET STEVENS

Reading Log

Use the Reading Log in the *Reader's and Writer's Notebook* to record your independent reading.

Common Core State Standards
Writing 3. Write narratives in which they recount a well-elaborated event or short sequence of events, include details to describe actions, thoughts, and feelings, use temporal words to signal event order, and provide a sense of closure. **Also Language 1.**

Let's Write It!

Key Features of a Narrative Poem

- has well-chosen words arranged in lines
- tells a brief story
- may have rhyming words

READING STREET ONLINE
GRAMMAR JAMMER
www.ReadingStreet.com

Narrative

Narrative Poem

A **narrative poem** is a poem that tells a story. The student model on the next page is an example of a narrative poem.

Writing Prompt Think about how creative thinking can solve a problem. Now write a narrative poem in which someone solves a problem.

Writer's Checklist

Remember, you should . . .

✓ tell a story in your poem.

✓ make the last words in some lines rhyme.

✓ use correct conventions in sentences.

✓ use verb tenses correctly.

Turtle's Race

Turtle wanted to win the race.

He could not run at a fast pace.

Turtle wanted to run to the gate.

He tried to roll on a roller skate.

The crowd said hi, wow, and yay.

Turtle quickly rolled away.

Then Turtle crossed the finish line.

He will yell, "Winning is fine!"

Past tense verbs end in **-ed. Future tense verbs** begin with **will**.

Writing Trait Conventions The sentences begin with a capital letter and end with a period.

Genre Read the **narrative poem** together. Hear the story.

Conventions

Verbs (Present, Past, Future)

Remember Verbs can tell about now. Verbs for the past usually add **-ed**.

 Verbs for the future begin with **will**.

Common Core State Standards

Literature 4. Describe how words and phrases (e.g., regular beats, alliteration, rhymes, repeated lines) supply rhythm and meaning in a story, poem, or song.

Science in Reading

Genre
Poetry

- Poetry has words written in lines with rhythm that is often repeated over and over.

- Rhyming poems end with the same sounds.

- Poetry helps you think about senses and feelings.

- Read "Do spiders stick to their own webs?" and "Do turtles leave their shells?" Look for words that rhyme in the poems.

- The setting is where a poem takes place. To compare the settings of poems, tell how the settings are alike and different.

- Read the poems. What is the setting of each poem? How are the settings of the two poems alike? How are the settings of the two poems different?

448

Do spiders stick to their own webs?

by Amy Goldman Koss

The spider weaves a sticky web
To capture bugs to eat.
What keeps the spider's sticky web
From sticking to her feet?

Spiderwebs are very tricky
Because not all the strands are sticky.
Unlike the passing hapless fly,
The spider knows which strands are dry.

But if by accident she stands
On any of the sticky strands,
She still would not get stuck, you see—
Her oily body slides off free.

Do turtles leave their shells?

by Amy Goldman Koss

The turtle's shell is cumbersome
And makes his movements slow.
Why doesn't he just take it off?
That's what I'd like to know.

Between his backbone and his shell
There is a strong connection.
It suits him well, he likes to have
His own built-in protection.

For if he tried to leave his shell,
He'd have to leave his bones as well.
So turtles really do not mind
That they can't leave their shells behind.

Let's **Think** About...

What words **rhyme** in the poems? What do you visualize when you hear these words?

Let's **Think** About...

How are the settings of the two poems alike and different?

Let's **Think** About...

Reading Across Texts What do *Anansi Goes Fishing* and "Do spiders stick to their own webs?" each say about spider webs?

Writing Across Texts Write a paragraph telling how spiders use webs.

Common Core State Standards
Language 5. Demonstrate understanding of word relationships and nuances in word meanings. **Also Literature 6., Foundational Skills 4.b., Speaking/Listening 4.**

**READING STREET ONLINE
VOCABULARY ACTIVITIES
www.ReadingStreet.com**

Vocabulary

An **antonym** is a word that means the opposite of another word. For example, *hot* is an antonym of *cold*.

Practice It! Complete each sentence by adding an antonym for the bold word.

1. The book was **good,** but the movie was ___.

2. My room was **messy,** but now it's ___.

Fluency

Expression Different characters talk and act in different ways. When reading aloud, read the words as if the character was speaking them. Be sure to understand the sentences.

Practice It! Read the sentences with expression.

1. Katie asked, "Is this a good place to fish?"

2. "Help!" the fly cried. "I am stuck in a web!"

450

Listening and Speaking

Use only the important ideas in a summary.

Summarize Information

When you summarize information, you retell it. You tell only what is important. You do not give lots of details. When you summarize, speak clearly in complete sentences. Tell the information in order. Do not speed through your summary. You want people to understand what you say. Listen attentively as others summarize information.

Practice It! Read a short article from a children's magazine. Summarize the article for the class. Use verbs for the past and present to make your summary clear.

Oral Vocabulary

Let's Talk About

Creative Ideas Leading to Surprises

- Share information about sharing with others.

- Share ideas about clever thinking.

READING STREET ONLINE
CONCEPT TALK VIDEO
www.ReadingStreet.com

452

Phonemic Awareness

Let's Listen for

Sounds

- Find five things that contain the long *i* sound.

- Find the light. Change the sound /l/ in *light* to the sound /n/. Say the new word.

- See the owl fly. Say the final sound in *fly*. Find something else that ends with the same sound.

READING STREET ONLINE
SOUND-SPELLING CARDS
www.ReadingStreet.com

454

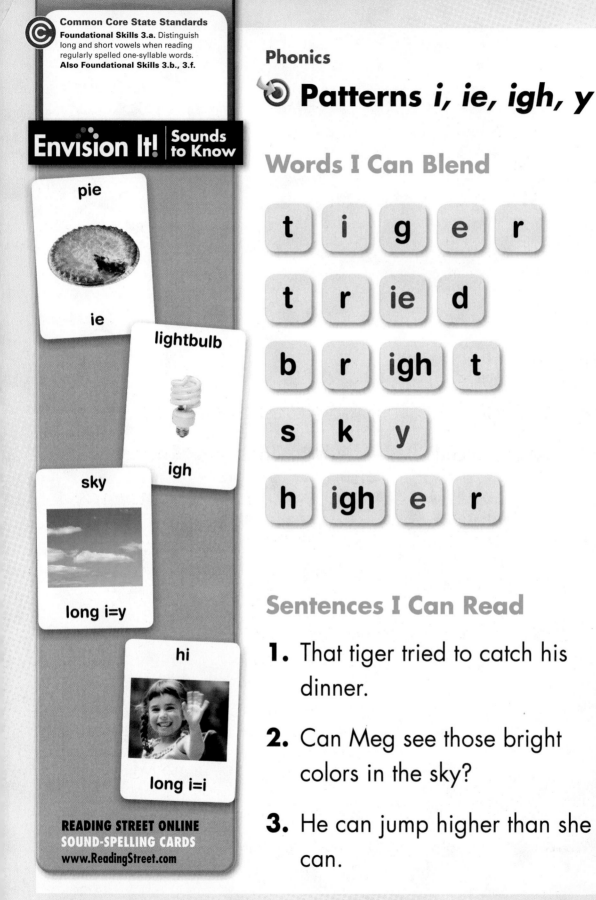

© Common Core State Standards
Foundational Skills 3.a. Distinguish
long and short vowels when reading
regularly spelled one-syllable words.
Also Foundational Skills 3.b., 3.f.

Envision It! | Sounds to Know

pie

ie

lightbulb

igh

sky

long i=y

hi

long i=i

READING STREET ONLINE
SOUND-SPELLING CARDS
www.ReadingStreet.com

Phonics

🔊 Patterns *i, ie, igh, y*

Words I Can Blend

t i g e r

t r ie d

b r igh t

s k y

h igh e r

Sentences I Can Read

1. That tiger tried to catch his dinner.

2. Can Meg see those bright colors in the sky?

3. He can jump higher than she can.

I Can Read!

One night their mom went to buy food alone. Three daughters sit at home with their dad. The youngest child cries, "Mom is kind in so many ways. We must find ways to repay her."

"What might we try?" sighs the oldest daughter. These three daughters lie awake half the night. All three try to find the right way to repay their mom. In the morning, the answer is still not in sight. Mom pleads, "You are the light of my life. Show love for me by being kind to others."

Rosa and Blanca

by Joe Hayes

illustrated by José Ortega

Genre **Realistic fiction** tells about made-up events that could happen in real life. Next you will read about Rosa and Blanca, two sisters with a clever idea.

Question of the Week

When does a creative idea lead to a surprise?

Once there were two sisters named Rosa and Blanca. They loved each other very much. If their mother sent Rosa to the store to buy flour for tortillas, Blanca would go with her. If their mother told Blanca to sweep the sidewalk in front of their house, Rosa would help her.

Their mother would always say, "My daughters are so good to one another. They make me very happy. I think I am the luckiest mother in the town. No. I am the luckiest mother in the country. No. I am the luckiest mother in the whole world!"

When Rosa and Blanca grew up, Rosa got married. She and her husband had three children. Blanca didn't get married. She lived alone.

One year Rosa planted a garden. Blanca planted a garden too. They planted corn and tomatoes and good hot *chiles*.

When the tomatoes were round and ripe, Rosa helped Blanca pick the tomatoes in her garden. Blanca helped Rosa pick the tomatoes in her garden.

That night Rosa thought, "My poor sister Blanca lives all alone. She has no one to help her make a living. I have a husband and helpful children. I will give her half of my tomatoes to sell in the market."

Rosa filled a basket with tomatoes. She started toward Blanca's house.

That very same night Blanca thought, "My poor sister Rosa has a husband and three children. There are five to feed in her house. I only have myself. I will give her half of my tomatoes to sell in the market."

Blanca filled a basket with tomatoes. She started toward Rosa's house. The night was dark. The two sisters did not see each other when they passed.

Rosa added her tomatoes to the pile in Blanca's kitchen. Blanca added her tomatoes to the pile in Rosa's kitchen.

The next day, Rosa looked at her pile of tomatoes. "*¡Vaya!*" she said. "How can I have so many tomatoes? Did my tomatoes have babies during the night?"

The next day Blanca looked at her pile of tomatoes. "¡Vaya!" she said. "How can I have so many tomatoes? Did my tomatoes have babies during the night?"

When the corn was ripe, Rosa helped Blanca pick her corn. Blanca helped Rosa pick her corn.

That night Rosa thought, "I will give half of my corn to Blanca to sell in the market."

That night Blanca thought, "I will give half of my corn to Rosa to sell in the market."

Each sister filled a basket with corn. Rosa went to Blanca's house. Blanca went to Rosa's house. The night was dark. They did not see each other when they passed.

Rosa added her corn to the corn in Blanca's house. Blanca added her corn to the corn in Rosa's house.

The next day Rosa said, "¡Vaya! How can I have so much corn? Did each ear invite a friend to spend the night?"

The next day Blanca said, "¡Vaya! How can I have so much corn? Did each ear invite a friend to spend the night?"

When the chiles were red and hot, Rosa helped Blanca pick her chiles. Blanca helped Rosa pick her chiles.

That night Rosa thought, "I will give Blanca half of my chiles to sell in the market."

That night Blanca thought, "I will give Rosa half of my chiles to sell in the market."

Each sister filled a basket with chiles.

Just then Rosa's youngest child started to cry. Rosa went to the child's room. She picked him up and rocked him.

Blanca was on her way to Rosa's house.

When Rosa's child went to sleep, Rosa picked up her basket of chiles. She started out the door. Blanca was coming in the door.

They both said, "¡Vaya!"

Rosa said, "Blanca, what are you doing? Why do you have that basket of chiles?"

Blanca said, "Rosa, what are you doing? Why do you have that basket of chiles?"

Rosa said, "I was going to give half of my chiles to you."

Blanca said, "But I was going to give half of my chiles to you!" Both sisters laughed.

Rosa said, "So that is why I still had so many tomatoes!"

Blanca said, "So that is why I still had so much corn!" The sisters hugged each other.

The next day Rosa and Blanca went to their mother's house. They told their mother what they had done.

Their old mother smiled and hugged her daughters. She said, "My daughters are so good to one another. They make me very happy. I think I am the luckiest mother in the town. No. I am the luckiest mother in the country. No. I am the luckiest mother in the whole world!"

Envision It! Retell

**READING STREET ONLINE
STORY SORT
www.ReadingStreet.com**

Think Critically

1. How is Rosa and Blanca's relationship the same as Pearl and Wagner's? Text to Text

2. Rosa and Blanca's mother says she is the luckiest mother "in the whole world." Why does the author tell this? Author's Purpose

3. When Rosa's child started to cry on page 467, what happened first? What happened next? Sequence

4. What did you predict the sisters would do with their vegetables? Tell why your prediction was correct or not. Predict and Set Purpose

5. Look Back and Write
Look back at page 462. How are the sisters alike and different? Provide evidence to support your answer.

Key Ideas and Details • Text Evidence

Meet the Author

Joe Hayes

Joe Hayes grew up listening to stories told by his father. He liked hearing stories so much that he decided he wanted to tell them too. Mr. Hayes began by telling stories to his own children. He soon realized that he liked telling stories to as many children as he could!

Mr. Hayes travels to many different places to share with children the stories he has learned. He has also published twenty books, many in English and Spanish.

Here are other books by Joe Hayes.

Use the Reading Log in the *Reader's and Writer's Notebook* to record your independent reading.

Common Core State Standards

Writing 3. Write narratives in which they recount a well-elaborated event or short sequence of events, include details to describe actions, thoughts, and feelings, use temporal words to signal event order, and provide a sense of closure. **Also Language 1.d.**

Let's Write It!

Key Features of Realistic Fiction

- tells about made-up people and events
- tells of events that could really happen
- has a beginning, middle, and end

READING STREET ONLINE
GRAMMAR JAMMER
www.ReadingStreet.com

Narrative

Realistic Fiction

Realistic fiction tells about made-up events that could really happen. The student model on the next page is an example of realistic fiction.

Writing Prompt Think about creative ideas that lead to surprises. Now write a realistic story about a character whose creative idea leads to a surprise.

Writer's Checklist

Remember, you should . . .

☑ make up a story that could really happen.

☑ use words that make your story interesting.

☑ write, read, and say verb tenses correctly.

Helping Out

Rita and Greta made a quick dinner for their busy family. They made sandwiches. They always like to cut the bread in shapes. Soon Mom walked in with two bags.

"I picked up dinner!" Mom announced. "We will eat."

"We made dinner!" Rita laughed.

"You are wonderful girls," said Mom.

Writing Trait Word Choice
Descriptive words *(quick, busy)* make the story clear and interesting.

Genre Realistic Fiction
The story includes events that seem real.

Past tense verbs
tell what happened. Say **picked** to hear the ending.

Conventions

 ## More About Verbs

Remember Use verbs for the present, the past, or the future. Some past tense verbs do not end in **-ed.** **made, said**

Common Core State Standards

Literature 2. Recount stories, including fables and folktales from diverse cultures, and determine their central message, lesson, or moral. **Also Literature 1.**

Social Studies in Reading

Genre
Fable

- A fable is a very short story that teaches a lesson.

- A fable's theme or lesson may be stated at the end of the story.

- Fables often use animals as the main characters.

- Read "The Crow and the Pitcher." Think about the lesson the fable is teaching.

The Crow and the Pitcher

a fable by Aesop retold by Eric Blair
illustrated by Laura Ovresat

There was once a thirsty crow. She had flown a long way looking for water.

The thirsty crow saw a pitcher of water and flew down to drink.

The pitcher had only a little water left at the bottom.

The crow put her beak into the pitcher. The water was so low she couldn't reach it.

474

But I must have water to drink. I can't fly any farther, thought the crow.

I know. I'll tip the pitcher over, she thought.

The thirsty crow beat the pitcher with her wings, but she wasn't strong enough to tip it.

Maybe I can break the pitcher. Then the water will flow, thought the crow.

Let's Think About...

What problem does the crow have? **Fable**

Let's Think About...

Is the crow able to tip the pitcher over? Why or why not? **Fable**

Let's **Think** About...

Why does the crow keep trying different ways of getting the water? **Fable**

She backed away to get a flying start. With all her might, the thirsty crow flew at the pitcher. She struck it with her pointed beak and claws, but the tired crow wasn't strong enough to break the pitcher.

Just as she was about to give up, the crow had another idea. She dropped a pebble into the pitcher. The water rose a little.

She dropped another and another. With each pebble, the water level rose more.

Soon the water reached the brim. The crow drank until she was no longer thirsty.

The crow was pleased with herself. By refusing to give up, she had solved her difficult problem.

Let's Think About...

What way finally works for the crow? **Fable**

Let's Think About...

Reading Across Texts What needs do the characters in *Rosa and Blanca* and "The Crow and the Pitcher" have? How do they meet their needs?

Writing Across Texts Would Rosa and Blanca have helped the crow get water? Write a sentence explaining your answer.

477

Common Core State Standards
Language 4.a. Use sentence-level context as a clue to the meaning of a word or phrase.
Also Foundational Skills 4., Speaking/Listening 4.

Let's
Learn
It!

READING STREET ONLINE VOCABULARY ACTIVITIES
www.ReadingStreet.com

Vocabulary

Words from another language may be included in stories. Pictures and words around a word from another language may help you understand the word.

Hola

Hola **is a Spanish word. It means "hello."**

Practice It! Read each sentence. Look for clues to the meanings of the Spanish words.

1. Luis had just finished painting his *casa*. His house was now white with green trim.

2. Grandma said "*muchas gracias*" many times as she thanked people for her gifts.

478

Listening and Speaking

Get Ready For Grade 3

Use sensory words in your descriptions.

Give a Description

When you give a description, use words that tell how something looks, sounds, feels, smells, or tastes. Speak clearly and at an appropriate rate. Then listeners will understand your description.

Practice It! Think of something you like a lot, such as a favorite meal, book, or toy. Describe it to the class, giving details that help them understand what you like about it. Remember to speak clearly so your friends can enjoy your description.

Fluency

Appropriate Phrasing

When reading, pause when you come to a comma. Stop for a short time when you come to a period or question mark.

Practice It! Read the sentences aloud.

Are we going to have a garden this year? I want to plant some corn, tomatoes, and beans. They will taste good.

Language 6. Use words and phrases acquired through conversations, reading and being read to, and responding to texts, including using adjectives and adverbs to describe (e.g., *When other kids are happy that makes me happy*).
Also Speaking/Listening 1.

Let's Talk About

Where Creative Ideas Come From

- Share information about research and working together.
- Share ideas about new ways of thinking.

READING STREET ONLINE
CONCEPT TALK VIDEO
www.ReadingStreet.com

481

Phonemic Awareness

Let's Listen for

Sounds

- Find two things to compare. Use words with *-er* and *-est* endings.

- Compare the birds. Which is the highest? Say each sound in *highest*.

- Compare the snowmen to the rabbits. Which are bigger? Say each sound in *bigger*.

READING STREET ONLINE
SOUND-SPELLING CARDS
www.ReadingStreet.com

483

Envision It! | **Sounds to Know**

taller
-er

smallest
-est

READING STREET ONLINE
SOUND-SPELLING CARDS
www.ReadingStreet.com

Comparative Endings
-er, -est

Words I Can Blend

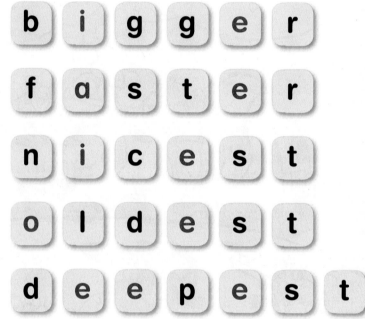

b i g g e r

f a s t e r

n i c e s t

o l d e s t

d e e p e s t

Sentences I Can Read

1. Luke's sister is bigger and faster than he is.

2. Tyler thinks he has the nicest teacher.

3. The oldest girl jumped in the deepest pool.

I Can Read!

Vicky's grandparents live down the street. Other family members live closer. Vicky's neighbor Lisa is Vicky's mom's sister. Vicky thinks Lisa is the kindest person she knows. Carlos is Lisa's only son. He is the funniest person. When Vicky has a question, family members help her find the smartest answer. Lisa has taught her the wisest ways to save money. Lisa's daughter Rachel helps her find the latest styles of clothes. Vicky spends hours with her family. She couldn't be happier!

You've learned

◎ Comparative Endings *-er, -est*

High-Frequency Words
clothes   hours   money
neighbor   only   question
taught

485

486

A Weed Is a Flower

The Life of George Washington Carver

by Aliki

 **Genre**

Biography tells about a real person's life, written by another person. It is an example of nonfiction. Next you will read the biography of George Washington Carver, a creative scientist.

Question of the Week

Where do creative ideas come from?

George Washington Carver was born in Missouri in 1860—more than a hundred years ago. It was a terrible time. Mean men rode silently in the night, kidnapping slaves from their owners and harming those who tried to stop them.

One night, a band of these men rode up to the farm of Moses Carver, who owned George and his mother, Mary. Everyone ran in fear. But before Mary could hide her baby, the men came and snatched them both, and rode away into the night.

Moses Carver sent a man to look for them. Mary was never found. But in a few days, the man returned with a small bundle wrapped in his coat and tied to the back of his saddle. It was the baby, George.

Moses and his wife, Susan, cared for Mary's children. George remained small and weak. But as he grew, they saw he was an unusual child. He wanted to know about everything around him. He asked about the rain, the flowers, and the insects. He asked questions the Carvers couldn't answer.

When he was very young, George kept a garden where he spent hours each day caring for his plants. If they weren't growing well, he found out why. Soon they were healthy and blooming. In winter he covered his plants to protect them. In spring he planted new seeds. George looked after each plant as though it was the only one in his garden.

Neighbors began to ask George's advice about their plants, and soon he was known as the Plant Doctor.

As time went on, George wondered about more and more things. He wanted to learn and yearned to go to school.

In the meantime, the slaves had been freed, but schools nearby were not open to blacks. So when he was ten, George left his brother, his garden, and the Carver farm and went off to find the answers to his questions.

Wherever George Washington Carver found schools, he stayed. He worked for people to earn his keep. He scrubbed their floors, washed their clothes, and baked their bread. Whatever George did, he did well. Even the smallest chore was important to him.

Some people took George in as their son. First he stayed with Mariah and Andy Watkins, who were like parents to him. Then he moved to Kansas and lived with "Aunt" Lucy and "Uncle" Seymour. They, too, loved this quiet boy who was so willing to help.

493

George worked hard for many years, always trying to save enough money for college. Other boys, who had parents to help them, were able to enter college much sooner than George. He was thirty before he had saved enough. Still, it was not that simple. Not all colleges would admit blacks, even if they had the money to pay.

George was not discouraged. He moved to Iowa and found a college which was glad to have a black student.

At college, George continued to work. He opened a laundry where he washed his schoolmates' clothes.

And, he continued to learn. His teachers and friends soon realized that this earnest young man was bursting with talents. He played the piano, he sang beautifully, and he was an outstanding painter. In fact, for a time he thought of becoming an artist.

496

But the more George thought of what he wanted to do, the more he wanted to help his people. And he remembered that his neighbors used to call him the Plant Doctor.

He had never forgotten his love for plants. In all the years he had wandered, he always had something growing in his room.

So, George Washington Carver chose to study agriculture. He learned about plants, flowers, and soil. He learned the names of the weeds. Even they were important to him. He often said: a weed is a flower growing in the wrong place.

He still asked questions. If no person or book could answer them, he found the answers himself. He experimented with his own plants, and found secrets no one else knew.

When George finished college, he began to teach. He was asked to go to Alabama, where a college for blacks needed his talent. It was there, at Tuskegee Institute, that George Washington Carver made his life.

In Alabama, Professor Carver taught his students and the poor black farmers, who earned their livelihood from the soil. He taught them how to make their crops grow better.

Most of the farmers raised cotton. But sometimes the crops were destroyed by rain or insects, and the farmers couldn't earn enough to eat.

Professor Carver told them to plant other things as well. Sweet potatoes and peanuts were good crops. They were easy to grow. He said that raising only cotton harmed the soil. It was better if different crops were planted each year.

The farmers did not want to listen. They were afraid to plant peanuts and sweet potatoes. They were sure that no one would buy them.

But Professor Carver had experimented in his laboratory. He had found that many things could be made from the sweet potato. He made soap, coffee, and starch. He made more than a hundred things from the sweet potato.

And even though people in those days called peanuts "monkey food," Professor Carver said they were good for people, too. Besides, he found that still more things could be made from the peanut. Paper, ink, shaving cream, sauces, linoleum, shampoo, and even milk! In fact, he made three hundred different products from the peanut.

Once, when important guests were expected at Tuskegee, Dr. Carver chose the menu. The guests sat around the table and enjoyed a meal of soup, creamed mock chicken, bread, salad, coffee, candy, cake, and ice cream. Imagine their surprise when they learned that the meal was made entirely from peanuts!

Slowly, the farmers listened to George Washington Carver. They planted peanuts and sweet potatoes. Before they knew it these became two of the most important crops in Alabama.

Soon the whole country knew about Dr. Carver and the great things he was doing. He was honored by Presidents and other important people. Every day, his mailbox bulged with letters from farmers and scientists who wanted his advice. He was offered great sums of money, which he turned down. Money was not important to him. He did not even bother to cash many of the checks he received.

Throughout his life, George Washington Carver asked nothing of others. He sought only to help. He lived alone and tended to his own needs. He washed his clothes and patched them, too. He used the soap he made and ate the food he grew.

Dr. Carver was asked to speak in many parts of the world, but he did not leave Tuskegee often. He had things to do. He continued to paint. He worked in his greenhouse and in his laboratory, where he discovered many things. He discovered that dyes could be made from plants, and colors from the Alabama clay. Even when he was over eighty and close to death, Dr. Carver kept working. Night after night, while the rest of the town lay asleep, a light still shone in his window.

The baby born with no hope for the future
grew into one of the great scientists of his country.
George Washington Carver, with his goodness and
devotion, helped not only his own people, but all
peoples of the world.

Common Core State Standards

Informational Text 1. Ask and answer such questions as *who, what, where, when, why,* and *how* to demonstrate understanding of key details in a text. **Also Informational Text 6.**

Envision It! | Retell

Think Critically

1. Think about *Rosa and Blanca* and this story. Which is fiction and which is nonfiction? Explain your answer. Text to Text

2. What did the author want you to know about George Washington Carver?

Author's Purpose

3. Find one opinion and one fact on pages 506–507. How can you tell the difference?

Fact and Opinion

4. How does Washington Carver pay for school? What does this tell you about him? Inferring

5. Look Back and Write
Look back at page 505. What did Washington Carver think about money? Provide evidence to support your answer.

Key Ideas and Details • Text Evidence

Meet the Author and Illustrator

Aliki

When Aliki writes a book, she often uses cartoons and draws funny characters talking in the margins. Her books are fun, but she does lots of research. "I spend many hours at my desk," she says. "Some books take three years to finish. That's why I call what I do hard fun."

Aliki grew up in Philadelphia, but her parents are from Greece. She speaks Greek as well as English. She prefers to use only her first name on her books.

Here are other books by Aliki.

Use the Reading Log in the *Reader's and Writer's Notebook* to record your independent reading.

Let's Write It!

Key Features of a Review

- explains what you liked or did not like in a selection
- tells your opinion about what you have read

READING STREET ONLINE
GRAMMAR JAMMER
www.ReadingStreet.com

Review

A review includes the writer's comments about a reading. The student model on the next page is an example of a review.

Writing Prompt Think about *A Weed Is a Flower.* Write a review. Tell what you found most interesting about George Washington Carver.

Writer's Checklist

Remember, you should . . .

☑ tell what you found interesting in the biography of Carver.

☑ write your idea and give supporting details.

☑ use verbs such as **am, is, are, was,** or **were**.

Review of <u>A Weed Is a Flower</u>

I liked reading that George Washington Carver had many talents. He was smart to make many things from sweet potatoes and peanuts. He could play the piano, sing, and paint. I liked finding out how he made paper from peanuts. I am sure he was a great scientist. I like this biography.

Writing Trait Organization
The paragraph has a main idea and supporting details.

The writer uses the **verbs am** and **was** correctly.

Genre
In this **review**, the writer comments about the biography.

Conventions

 Verbs Am, Is, Are, Was, and Were

Remember Am, **is**, and **are** tell about now.

 Was and **were** tell about the past.

21st Century Skills
INTERNET GUY

Use a child-friendly search engine that will answer questions. This makes it easy to find things. Just type in your question.

- A search engine is a research tool. It guides you to information on the Internet.

- A search engine can find Web sites on a topic.

- You use keywords to begin a search using a search engine.

- Read "What's Made from Corn?" Use the text and the pictures to learn about search engines.

What's Made from Corn?

If you are writing a report, you can use the Internet to help find information. Maria wants to give a report on how corn is used every day. She does an Internet search using a search engine. First, Maria brainstorms a list of keywords about her topic. These can be single words or groups of words that she will type into the search window of a search engine. Maria comes up with these keywords:

> **Corn**
>
> **Uses of corn**
>
> **How we use corn**

She can type any of these into a search engine window and then click the Search button. After a few seconds, she gets a list of Web sites.

7. Fruits and Vegetables: Corn

Corn now available to buy! Online shopping is easy at our huge shopping mall.

8. Things to Do with Corn!

Products that use **corn.** Fun classroom projects for planting, growing, and harvesting corn.

9. Cool Products Made from Corn

Everything you always wanted to know about **corn.**

10. How to Grow Corn

Tips on growing different kinds of **corn.**

Maria uses her mouse and the scroll bar to go through the list. When Maria gets to the ninth item, she stops. This sounds like a helpful Web site.

Maria clicks on the link <u>Cool Products Made from Corn</u>. This link has many pictures and descriptions. The next thing Maria sees on her computer screen is:

File   Edit   View   Favorites   Tools   Help

http://www.url.here

Cool Products Made from Corn

- Corn can be used to make knives, forks, and spoons. Corn can be used to make plates, diapers, milk jugs, razors, and golf tees. All these things dissolve when put into the garbage. This helps the environment.

- Corn can be made into "packing peanuts." Packing peanuts are used to protect objects packed in boxes. These peanuts dissolve in water.

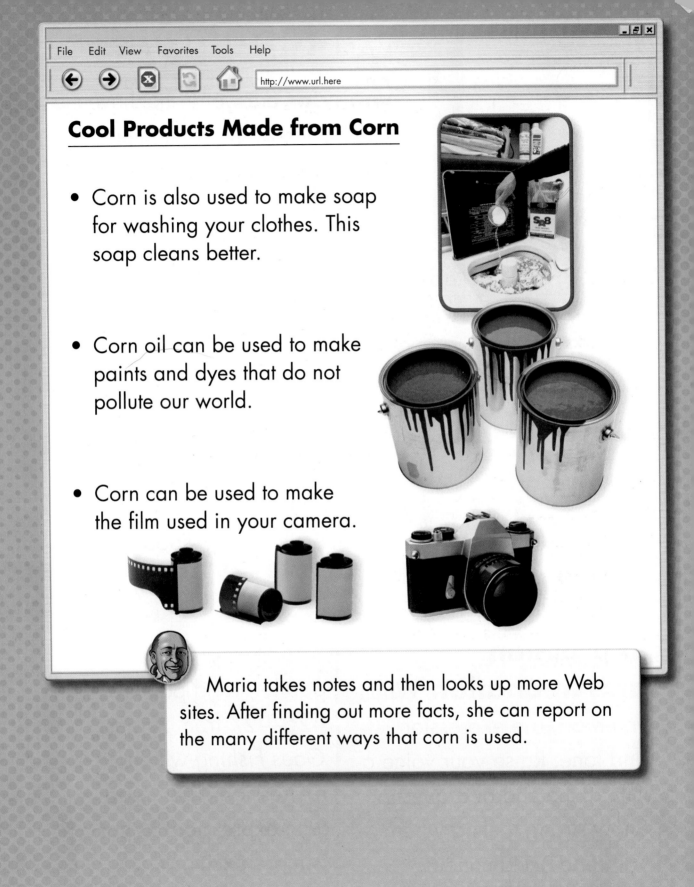

Cool Products Made from Corn

- Corn is also used to make soap for washing your clothes. This soap cleans better.

- Corn oil can be used to make paints and dyes that do not pollute our world.

- Corn can be used to make the film used in your camera.

Maria takes notes and then looks up more Web sites. After finding out more facts, she can report on the many different ways that corn is used.

Common Core State Standards
Foundational Skills 4.b. Read on-level text orally with accuracy, appropriate rate, and expression on successive readings.

Let's Learn It!

READING STREET ONLINE
VOCABULARY ACTIVITIES
www.ReadingStreet.com

Vocabulary

Synonyms are words that have the same or almost the same meaning. For example, *happy* and *glad* are synonyms.

Practice It! Read each sentence. Choose the synonym of the bold word. Then use the synonyms in your own sentences.

1. The chef **chopped** the carrots.   made   cut

2. Which kitchen **utensil** do you use to sift flour?   spoon   tool

Fluency

Expression and Intonation When you read, use expression and tone. Raise your voice a little at the end of a question. Show strong feeling when you read exclamations.

Practice It! With a partner, read pages 426–427 from *Anansi Goes Fishing* with no expression. Then read with expression. What is more exciting?

Media Literacy

Get Ready For Grade 3

Describe how sounds and graphics are used to create media messages.

Describe Media Techniques

Media, such as Internet sites and television, often uses sound and graphics, or pictures. The sounds and graphics may tell stories or give information. Sometimes you will see and hear opinions as well as facts. Listen and watch media carefully.

Practice It! Compare a story you saw or heard in the media with a story you read in the book. Think about the way pictures and words are presented. Tell how the media stories and the stories in books are alike. Tell how they are different.

Tips

Speaking . . .

• Describe how words, images, graphics, and sounds work together in media to affect meaning.

agriculture • collar

Aa

astronaut

Bb

Cc

cactus

agriculture (ag ruh KUL cher) **Agriculture** is farming and growing crops. *NOUN*

armadillo (ar muh DIL oh) An **armadillo** is an animal that has a hard, bony covering. *NOUN*

astronaut (ASS truh nawt) An **astronaut** is a person who has been trained to fly in a spacecraft. While in space, **astronauts** repair space stations and do experiments. *NOUN*

brave (BRAYV) If you are **brave,** you are not afraid: The **brave** girl pulled her little brother away from the burning leaves. *ADJECTIVE*

cactus (KAK tuhss) A **cactus** is a plant with sharp parts but no leaves: Most **cactuses** grow in very hot, dry areas of North and South America. Many have bright flowers. *NOUN*

chiles (CHIL ayz) **Chiles** are a green or red pepper with a hot taste. *NOUN*

climate (KLY mit) **Climate** is the kind of weather a place has. *NOUN*

collar (KOL er) A **collar** is a band that is put around the neck of a dog or other pet. **Collars** can be made of leather or plastic. *NOUN*

college (KOL ij) **College** is the school that you go to after high school: After I finish high school, I plan to go to **college** to become a teacher. *NOUN*

cousins (KUH zins) Your **cousins** are the children of your aunt or uncle. *NOUN*

coyote (ky OH tee *or* KY oht) A **coyote** is a small animal that looks something like a wolf: **Coyotes** have light yellow fur and bushy tails. *NOUN*

coyote

creature (KREE chur) A **creature** is a living being: Many **creatures** live in the forest. *NOUN*

Dd

dangerous (DAYN jer uhss) Something that is **dangerous** is not safe: Skating on thin ice is **dangerous.** *ADJECTIVE*

delicious (di LISH uhss) When something is **delicious,** it tastes or smells very good: The cookies were **delicious.** *ADJECTIVE*

desert (DEZ ert) A **desert** is a place without water or trees but with a lot of sand. It is usually hot. *NOUN*

desert

drooled (DROOLD) To **drool** is to let saliva run from the mouth like a baby sometimes does: The dog **drooled** when it saw the bone. *VERB*

519

Ee

electricity (i lek TRISS uh tee) **Electricity** is a kind of energy that makes light and heat. **Electricity** also runs motors. **Electricity** makes light bulbs shine, radios and televisions play, and cars start. *NOUN*

envelope (EN vuh lohp) An **envelope** is a folded paper cover. An **envelope** is used to mail a letter or something else that is flat. *NOUN*

excitement (ek SYT muhnt) **Excitement** happens when you have very strong, happy feelings about something that you like. *NOUN*

experiment (ek SPEER uh ment) An **experiment** is a test to find out something: We do **experiments** in science class. *NOUN*

Ff

fault (FAWLT) If something is your **fault,** you are to blame for it. *NOUN*

Gg

gnaws (NAWZ) When an animal **gnaws,** it is biting and wearing away by biting: The brown mouse **gnaws** the cheese. *VERB*

grateful (GRAYT fuhl) If you are **grateful** for something, you are thankful for it. *ADJECTIVE*

gravity (GRAV uh tee) **Gravity** is the natural force that causes objects to move toward the center of the Earth. **Gravity** causes objects to have weight. *NOUN*

greenhouse (GREEN howss) A **greenhouse** is a building with a glass or plastic roof and sides. A **greenhouse** is kept warm and full of light for growing plants. *NOUN*

greenhouse

groaned (GROHND) To **groan** is to make a low sound showing that you are in pain or are unhappy about something: We all **groaned** when it started to rain during recess. *VERB*

Hh

harsh (HARSH) To be **harsh** is to be rough, unpleasant, and unfriendly: The **harsh** weather made us stay indoors. *ADJECTIVE*

honest (ON ist) Someone who is **honest** does not lie, cheat, or steal. *ADJECTIVE*

hurricanes (HUR uh kains) A **hurricane** is a violent storm with strong winds: The Florida **hurricanes** blew the roofs off many houses. *NOUN*

Jj

justice (JUHS tis) **Justice** happens when things are right and fair. *NOUN*

Ll

laboratory (LAB ruh tor ee) A **laboratory** is a room where scientists work and do experiments and tests. *NOUN*

lanterns • musician

lantern

lanterns (LAN ternz) **Lanterns** are portable lamps with coverings around them to protect them from wind and rain. *NOUN*

lawyer (LOI er) A **lawyer** is someone who is trained to give people advice about the law. A **lawyer** helps people when they go to court. *NOUN*

lazy (LAY zee) If a person is **lazy,** he or she does not want to work hard or to move fast: The **lazy** cat lay on the rug all day. *ADJECTIVE*

luckiest (LUHK ee est) The **luckiest** person is the one who has had the best fortune. *ADJECTIVE*

Mm

meadow (MED oh) A **meadow** is a piece of land where grass grows: There are sheep in the **meadow.** *NOUN*

mill (MIL) A **mill** is a building in which grain is ground into flour or meal. *NOUN*

monsters (MON sterz) **Monsters** are make-believe people or animals that are scary. In stories, some **monsters** are friendly, and others are not: Dragons are **monsters.** *NOUN*

musician (myoo ZISH uhn) A **musician** is a person who sings, plays, or writes music. *NOUN*

Nn

narrator (NAIR ayt or) A **narrator** is a person who tells a story or play. In a play, a **narrator** keeps the action moving. *NOUN*

noticed (NOH tisd) To **notice** means to see something or become aware of it: The boys **noticed** a strange smell near the cave. *VERB*

Pp

parents (PAIR ents) Your **parents** are your mother and father. *NOUN*

persimmons

persimmons (puhr SIM uhns) **Persimmons** are round yellow and orange fruits about the size of plums. *NOUN*

photograph (FOH tuh graf) A **photograph** is a picture you make with a camera. *NOUN*

promise (PROM iss) If you make a **promise** to do something, you are giving your word that you will do it. *NOUN*

Rr

relatives (REL uh tivs) Your **relatives** are the people who belong to the same family as you do: Your mother, sister, and cousin are all your **relatives.** *NOUN*

resources (REE sor sez) **Resources** are things people need and use, such as food, water, and building materials. *NOUN*

523

robbers (ROB ers) **Robbers** are people who rob or steal: The police chased the bank **robbers.** *NOUN*

robots

robot (ROH bot *or* ROH BUHT) A **robot** is a machine that is run by a computer. **Robots** help people do work. **Robots** can look like people. *NOUN*

Ss

scarce (SKAIRSS) If something is **scarce,** it is hard to find because there is so little of it: Empty seats were **scarce** at the sold-out show. *ADJECTIVE*

scarcity (SKAIR suh tee) **Scarcity** happens when there is not enough of something for everyone who wants it: Dry weather damaged the farmers' crops and caused a **scarcity** of corn. *NOUN*

shivered (SHIV erd) To **shiver** is to shake with cold, fear, or excitement: I **shivered** in the cold wind. *VERB*

shuttle (SHUHT uhl) A **shuttle** is a spacecraft with wings, which can orbit the Earth, land like an airplane, and be used again. *NOUN*

slipped (SLIPT) When you **slip,** you slide suddenly and unexpectedly: She **slipped** on the ice. *VERB*

smudged (SMUDJD) If something is **smudged,** it is marked with a dirty streak. *ADJECTIVE*

snuggled

Tt

snorted (SNOR ted) To **snort** means to breathe noisily through the nose: Her brother **snorted** when he laughed. *VERB*

snuggled (SNUHG uhld) To **snuggle** is to lie closely and comfortably together; cuddle: The kittens **snuggled** together in the basket. *VERB*

telescope (TEL uh skohp) A **telescope** is something you look through to make things far away seem nearer and larger: We looked at the moon through a **telescope.** *NOUN*

tortillas (tor TEE uhs) **Tortillas** are thin, flat, round breads usually made of cornmeal. *NOUN*

trade-off (TRAYD off) You make a **trade-off** when you give up one thing you want for something else you want even more. *NOUN*

trash

Ww

trash (TRASH) **Trash** is anything of no use or that is worn out. **Trash** is garbage or things to be thrown away. *NOUN*

wad (WOD) A **wad** is a small, soft ball or chunk of something: She threw a **wad** of paper in the wastebasket. *NOUN*

weave (WEEV) To **weave** is to form threads into cloth. *VERB*

Unit 1
The Twin Club

beautiful
country
friend
front
someone
somewhere

Exploring Space with an Astronaut

everywhere
live
machines
move
woman
work
world

Henry and Mudge and the Starry Night

bear
build
couldn't
father
love
mother
straight

A Walk in the Desert

animals
early
eyes
full
warm
water

The Strongest One

gone
learn
often
pieces
though
together
very

Unit 2

Tara and Tiree, Fearless Friends

break
family
heard
listen
once
pull

Abraham Lincoln

certainly
either
great
laugh
second
worst
you're

Scarcity

above
ago
enough
toward
whole
word

The Bremen Town Musicians

bought
people
pleasant
probably
scared
shall
sign

One Good Turn Deserves Another

behind
brought
door
everybody
minute
promise
sorry

Unit 3
Pearl and Wagner

guess
pretty
science
shoe
village
watch
won

Dear Juno

answer
company
faraway
parents
picture
school
wash

Anansi Goes Fishing

been
believe
caught
finally
today
tomorrow
whatever

Rosa and Blanca

alone
buy
daughters
half
many
their
youngest

A Weed Is a Flower

clothes
hours
money
neighbor
only
question
taught

529

Acknowledgments

Text

Grateful acknowledgment is made to the following for copyrighted material:

Aladdin Paperbacks an imprint of Simon & Schuster Children's Publishing Division

Reprinted with permission of Aladdin Paperbacks, an imprint of Simon & Schuster Children's Publishing Division. All rights reserved. From *Tara And Tiree, Fearless Friends: A True Story* Andrew Clements. Text copyright © 2002 by Andrew Clements.

Alfred A. Knopf a div of Random House, Inc

From *Silly & Sillier: Read-Aloud Rhymes From Around The World* by Judy Sierra and illus. by Valeri Gorbachev, copyright © 2002 by Judy Sierra. Illustrations copyright © 2002 by Valeri Gorbachev. Used by permission of Alfred A. Knopf, an imprint of Random House Children's Books, a division of Random House, Inc.

Alloy, Inc

"A Walk in the Desert" by Caroline Arnold. Copyright © 1990 by Alloy Entertainment and Al Jarnow. Reprinted by permission. All rights reserved.

Capstone Press

"Scarcity" by Janeen R. Adil. Copyright © 2006 by Capstone Press. Used by permission. All rights reserved.

Columbia University Press

"Rain Forests (Originally titled Forests)" from *The Columbia Electronic Encyclopedia, 6th Edition*. New York: Columbia University Press, Copyright © 2005. Used by permission.

Dial Books for Young Readers a div of Penguin Group (USA)

"Do Spiders Stick to Their Own Webs?" from *Where Do Fish Go In Winter and Other Great Mysteries* by Amy Goldman Koss, copyright © 1987 by Amy Goldman Koss. . ''Pearl and Wagner" from *Pearl And Wagner: Two Good Friends* by Kate McMullan, illustrations by R.W. Alley. Text copyright © 2003 by Kate McMullan, Illustrations copyright © 2003 by R.W. Alley. "The Strongest Once," *from Pushing Up the Sky* by Joseph Bruchac, copyright © 2000 by Joseph Bruchac, text. Used by permission of Dial Books for Young Readers, A Division of Penguin Young Readers Group, A Member of Penguin Group (USA) Inc., 345 Hudson Street, New York, NY 10014. All rights reserved.

Enslow Publishers, Inc

From *Exploring Space with an Astronaut* by Patricia J. Murphy. Copyright © 2004 by Enslow Publishers, Inc. Published by Enslow Publishers, Inc., Berkeley Heights, NJ. Used by permission of Enslow Publishers, Inc. All rights reserved.

Henry Holt and Company, LLC

"The 1st Day of School" and "The 179th Day of School" from *Lunch Box Mail and Other Poems* by Jenny Whitehead. © 2001 by Jenny Whitehead. Reprinted by permission of Henry Holt and Company, LLC.

Holiday House, Inc

"Anansi Goes Fishing" by Eric A. Kimmel, illustrated by Janet Stevens. Text copyright © 1992 by Eric A. Kimmel. Illustrations copyright © 1992 by Janet Stevens. All rights reserved. Reprinted by permission of Holiday House, Inc.

Joe Hayes

"Rosa and Blanca" by Joe Hayes, illustrated by Jose Ortega, 1993. Used by permission of Joe Hayes.

Millbrook Press a div of Learner Publishing Group

From *Many Ways To Be A Soldier* by Wendy Pfeffer. Text copyright © 2008 by Wendy Pfeffer. Used with the permission of Millbrook Press, a division of Lerner Publishing Group, Inc. All rights reserved. No Part of this text excerpt may be used or reproduced in any manner whatsoever without the prior written permission of Learner Publishing Group, Inc.

Ohio Corn Marketing Program

"What's Made from Corn?" (Originally titled Products Made from Corn) from *Www.Ohiocorn.Org.* Used by permission.

Picture Window Books/Compass Point Books

"The Crow and the Pitcher" retold by Eric Blair. Copyright © 2004 by Compass Point Books. All rights reserved. Used by permission.

Scholastic, Inc

From *Easy-To-Read Folk & Fairy Tale Plays* by Carol Pugliano. Scholastic Inc/Teaching Resources. Copyright © 1997 by Carol Pugliano. Reprinted by permission.

Simon & Schuster Books for Young Readers an imprint of Simon & Schuster Children's Division

From *Henry And Mudge And The Starry Night* by Cynthia Rylant, illustrated by Sucie Stevenson. Text copyright © 1998 by Cynthia Rylant, Illustrations copyright © 1998 by Sucie Stevenson. From *A Weed is a Flower* by Aliki Brandenberg. Text copyright © 1965, 1988 by Aliki Brandenberg. Reprinted with permission of Simon & Schuster Books for Young Readers, an imprint of Simon & Schuster Children's Publishing Division. All rights reserved.

Viking Children's Books a Div of Penguin Group (USA)

"Dear Juno" from *Dear Juno* by Soyung Pak. Text copyright © 1999 by Soyung Pak, Illustrations copyright © 1999 by Susan Kathleen Hartung. Used by permission of Viking Children's Books, a division of Penguin Young Readers Group, a member of Penguin Group (USA) Inc., 375 Hudson Street, New York, NY 10014 and Dystel & Goderich Literary Management, Inc. All rights reserved.

Note: Every effort has been made to locate the copyright owner of material reproduced on this component. Omissions brought to our attention will be corrected in subsequent editions.

Cover: (C)©Jupiterimages/Getty Images, (TR) ©Kim Karpeles/Alamy Images, (TC) ©lassendesignen/Fotolia, (TL) TongRo Image Stock, (BC) ©Benshot/Fotolia

Illustrations

E11-E115 Robert Neubecker; E118-I27 John Haslam; 16 Dani Jones; 26-46 Jana Christy; 48 Stephen Gilpin; 78 Gabriel Carranza; 110 Bill McGuire; 146 Nathan Hale; 156-175 David Diaz; 179 Derek Grinnell; 182 Victor Rivas; 192-206 Scott Gustafson; 214 Matt Luxich; 224, 230-236 Stephen Costanza; 244 Orlando Ramirez; 274 Ethan Long; 280-295 Jon Goodell; 307-310 Dylan T. Weeks; 308 Mick Reid; 320, 322-334 Will Terry; 340-343 Dan Andreasen; 342 Jennifer Zivoin; 368-37l Paul Eric Roca; 374 Erwin Haya; 406 Doug Holgate; 410-415 Paul Weiner; 440 Scott R. Brooks; 468 Steve Simpson; 474-477 Laura Ovresat

Photographs

Photo locators denoted as follows: Top (T), Center (C), Bottom (B), Left (L), Right (R), Background (Bkgd)
CVR (Blue sky) TongRo Image Stock/Fotosearch; **CVR** (Plants) Benshot/Fotolia; **CVR** (Garden) Jupiter Images/ Getty Images; **4** (TL), **18** Stephen Frink/Corbis; **8** (TL) Juniors Bildarchiv/Alamy; **12** (TL) Roger Bamber/Alamy; **16** (C) ellenamani/Fotolia; **20** (Bkgrd) Powered by Light/ Alan Spencer/Alamy; **20** (BL) Patrik Giardino/Corbis; **21** (BR) Tom & Dee Ann McCarthy/Corbis; **24** (TL) GRIN/NASA; **24** (TCL) ellenamani/Fotolia; **24** (BL) Vittorio Bruno/Shutterstock; **24** (BCL) Jupiter Images; **24** (CL) Carleton Chinner/Shutterstock; **52** (Bkgrd) Shilo Sports/Getty Images; **52** (B) George Hall/Corbis; **53** Deco/Alamy; **56** (CL) David R. Frazier/Photolibrary/ Alamy; **56** (TCL) Getty Images; **56** (BL) Jupiter Images/ Getty Images; **58** (TL) Getty Images; **58** (Bkgrd) Corbis; **58** (C) Getty Images; **58** (CR) Getty Images; **59, 60, 61** (B) (T), **62** (BL), (BR), **63** (B), (T), **64, 65, 66** (TR) (Bkgrd), **68** (C) (T), **69** (Bkgrd), (CR), **70–71, 72, 81** NASA; **68** (Bkgrd) Getty Images; **73** (BL) Getty Images; **74** Richard T. Nowitz/Corbis; **76** (C) Anderson Ross/Getty Images; **77** (TR) Corbis; **77** (B), (CR), **78** (BR), **79** (TL) Richard T. Nowitz/Corbis; **77** (BR) Joseph Sohm/ ChromoSohm Inc/Corbis; **79** (TR) Franz-MarcFrei/ Corbis; **80** (T) John Foxx/Getty Images; **80** (TC) Image Source/Getty Images; **82** (Bkgrd) Jim Ballard/Getty Images; **83** (BR) Joe McDonald/Corbis; **83** (CR) Nigel J.Dennis/Gallo Images/Corbis; **83** (TC) Michael & Patricia Fogden/Corbis; **86** (TL) Roderick Chen/Getty Images; **86** (TR) Getty Images; **112** (CR) noyes3/Fotolia; **112** (CL) vrabelpeter1/Fotolia; **114** George H. H. Huey/Corbis; **115** (BC) Getty Images; **115** (TC) Brand X Pictures/ PunchStock; **118** (BCL) Allen Brown/dbimages/Alamy; **118** (TL) Andrea Matone/Alamy; **118** (TCL) Joe Fox Dublin/Alamy; **118** (CL) Stock4B/Getty Images; **120–121** Maryellen Baker/Botanica/Getty Images; **122** (Bkgrd) Visions of America/Joe Sohm/Getty Images; **122** (BL) Anton Foltin/Shutterstock; **122** (BR) Nickolay Stanev/Shutterstock; **123** (R), **140** (TC) Robert Van Der Hilst/Getty Images; **124** (Bkgrd) Paul McCormick/ Getty Images; **125** (BC) Emmanuel LATTES/Alamy; **125** (BR) Bates Littlehales/National Geographic Stock/ Getty Images; **125** (CR) Gary W.Carter/Corbis; **125** (C) ©Jim David/Shutterstock; **126** (CR) Charles C. Place/ Getty Images; **126** (TC) Steve Byland/Fotolia; **127** (TR), **140** (TCL) David Aubrey/Getty Images; **128** (Bkgrd) Arthur S. Aubry/Getty Images; **128** (C) Ariel Bravy/ Shutterstock; **129** (BR), **140** (CL) David A. Northcott/ Corbis; **129** (TR) George D. Lepp/Corbis; **129** (CL) Joe McDonald/Corbis; **130** (BL) Farrell Grehan/Corbis; **130** (BR) Shai Ginott/Corbis; **130** (BL) Farrell Grehan/Corbis; **130** (Bkgrd) Getty Images; **131** (B) Alamy; **132** (Bkgrd) Joe McDonald/Corbis; **133** (BL) Jonathan Blair/National Geographic Stock/Getty Images; **133** (BR) Jeremy Woodhouse/Getty Images; **134** (Bkgrd) (BL) Getty Images; **134** (BR) Michael & Patricia Fogden/Corbis; **135** (TL) Getty Images; **135** (BR), **140** (CCL) Jeremy Woodhouse/ Getty Images; **135** (TR) Mel Yates/Getty Images; **136** (BL)

Adam James/Alamy; **136** (BR) Layne Kennedy/Corbis; **137** (TC), **140** (BCL) Matthias Clamer/Getty Images; **138–139** (Bkgd), **140** (BL) Jean-luc Cochonneau/Alamy; **138** (CL) Tim Flach/Getty Images; **138** (CR) William J Hebert/Getty Images; **139** (CR) blickwinkel/Alamy; **139** (BC) Ira Rubin/ Getty Images; **139** (TL) Warren Jacobi/Corbis; **140** (BR) Ariel Bravy/Shutterstock; **141** (TR) Steve Byland/Fotolia; **142** (BL) Maryellen Baker/Botanica; **146** (BL) Theo Allofs/Corbis; **146** (CL) Gary Braasch/Corbis; **147** (CL) Tom Brakefield/Corbis; **147** (TL) Bill Varie/Corbis; **150** (BC) Ron Watts/Corbis; **150** (BC) Galyna Andrushko/ Fotolia; **150** (TC) Martin Harvey/Photolibrary/Getty Images; **154** (BL) Tom Brakefield/Corbis; **154** (BR) Jupiter Images; **154** (CL) Cbpix/Fotolia; **178** (Bkgrd), **179** (BR) Tom Brakefield/Corbis; **180** (T) Getty Images/ Flickr Open; **180** (BL) John H. Hoffman/Photoshot; **181** Theo Allofs/Corbis; **182** (TL) Peter Arnold/Getty Images; **182** (TR) Getty Images; **184** Juniors Bildarchiv/ Alamy; **186** Stocktrek/Getty Images; **187** (BC) Ravell Call/ Hulton Archive/Getty Images; **187** (C) Larry W. Smith/ epa/Corbis; **190** (TR) Getty Images/Glowimages; **190** (CL) Laura Ashley/Alamy; **190** (TL) Blend Images/Alamy; **212** atref/Shutterstock; **213** (CL) Tom Bear/Aurora Creative/ Getty Images; **213** (BC) Tom Nebbia/Corbis; **213** (BL) Gambarini Mauricio/dpa/Corbis; **213** (TL) Andrea Comas/Corbis; **214–215** (Bkgrd) Owen Franken/Corbis; **214** (CL) Shamil Zhumatov/Corbis; **214** (CR) Armando Arorizo/Corbis; **214** (TR) Vaughn Youtz/Corbis; **215** Ralf-Finn Hestoft/Corbis; **218–219** (Bkgrd) Bernard Annebicque/Sygma/Corbis; **218** (B) Jennifer Brown/Star Ledger/Corbis; **218** (T) LWA-Sharie Kennedy/Corbis; **236** (BC) Corbis; **237** (BR) Bettmann/Corbis; **237** (C) Corbis; **248** (BC) Peter Vadnal/Corbis; **248–249** (Bkgrd) Stock Photos/zefa/Corbis; **248** (TR) James Leynse/Corbis; **248** (BC) Andre Jenny/Alamy; **252** (CR) Radius Images; **252** (CL) MIXACo., Ltd/Alamy; **252** (TL) Olivier Asselin/ Alamy; **254–255, 268** (TL) Chris Livingston/Getty Images; **258** Wayne Eastep/Getty Images; **259** Bill Bachman/ Alamy; **260** Jupiter Images; **260, 268** (TCL) Jupiter Images; **261, 270** David R. Frazier/Photolibrary, Inc./Alamy; **262, 268** (CL) Phil Klein/Corbis; **263, 268** (CCL) Jack Hollingsworth/Thinkstock; **266–267, 268** (BL) Owen Franken/Corbis; **273** (CL) Photos to Go; **273** (CR) Jade/ Blend Images/Getty Images; **274** (CL) VStock/Photos to Go; **274** (CR) Jonathan Nourok/Photo Edit, Inc.; **275** Felicia Martinez/PhotoEdit, Inc.; **278–279** Ariel Skelley/Corbis; **279** (B) Michael Pole/Corbis; **279** (T) Paul Harris/Getty Images; **282** (BL) Photas Ltd/Alamy; **282** (CR) Getty Images; **282** (TL) DLILLC/Corbis; **314** David Katzenstein/Corbis; **314–315** Gemstone Images/ Stock Photos/Glowimages; **315** (T) Design Pics Inc/ Alamy; **315** (B) Stewart Cohen/Corbis; **318** (TL) Mike Dobel/Alamy; **318** (CL) Image Alchemy/Alamy; **346** Roger Bamber/Alamy; **348** imagebroker/Alamy; **349** (CR) Blend Images/Superstock; **349** (BC) Jim Cummins/Getty Images; **352** (CL) Morales Morales/Photolibrary/Getty Images; **352** (CR) Ralph A. Clevenger/Corbis; **352** (BR) David R. Frazier/Photolibrary, Inc./Alamy; **380** (L) Purestock/Getty Images; **380** (R) 4EyesPhotography/ Getty Images; **382** (T) Kitt Cooper-Smith/Alamy; **382** (B) Photo Alto/James Hardy/Getty Images; **386** (CR) Getty Images; **386** (CL) Benjamin Rondel/Corbis; **386** (TL) Terrance Klassen/Alamy; **418–419** (Bkgrd) Karl Ammann/ Nature Picture Library; **418** (T) Francois Gohier/Science Source; **418** (B) Masterfile; **422** Getty Images; **448** (B) PBNJ Productions/Corbis; **448** (T) GK Hart/Vikki Hart/